INTO EDEN

Elements of Emancipation

Redpanther/John F. Burnett

Cover Painting by John F. Burnett

authorHOUSE®

AuthorHouse™
1663 Liberty Drive
Bloomington, IN 47403
www.authorhouse.com
Phone: 1-800-839-8640

Published by AuthorHouse 02/12/2015

ISBN: 978-1-4969-3142-9 (sc)
ISBN: 978-1-4969-3141-2 (hc)
ISBN: 978-1-4969-3140-5 (e)

Library of Congress Control Number: 2014913886

Print information available on the last page.

*Any people depicted in stock imagery provided by Thinkstock are models,
and such images are being used for illustrative purposes only.
Certain stock imagery © Thinkstock.*

This book is printed on acid-free paper.

John Burnett is the result of self-education, put into practice. The result of this is a freer life than most people in this so-called Land of the Free could even imagine. In addition to writing, he works as a landscape contractor. Of redneck descent, he has spent much time in the backwoods of Northern and Central California since the age of 3.

Bad, BAD redneck (the author)
in traditional tribal dress

Bad, BAD cougar-kitty
with Bart Culver

"Being alive in nature, before our abstraction from it, must have involved a perception and contact that we can scarcely comprehend from our levels of anguish and alienation." (John Zerzan, Elements of Refusal, pg. 31)

My commentary (from direct experience): It is not comprehensible.

"The savage mind totalizes."
(Claude Levi-Strauss, The Savage Mind, pg. 245)

"At the core of our system is a moral decay that is tolerated only because the cleansing of its Augean stables is too traumatic to contemplate." (Robert Skidelsky and Edward Sidelsky, How Much is Enough?)

Table of Contents

Foreword

A great deal of this book covers normal human nature – what it is, what enables it, and how it originally evolved. And then – what has been done to it, and how to clean up the mess. What we are dealing with today is **damaged** human nature, and the solution will require understanding this damage and how deep it goes.

The word "normal" will raise some hackles. What I mean here is not the "norm" in a very sick society (1), but "normal" as a medical doctor would use the word – free from significant or major pathology.

This book is a tool kit. You may disagree with some of the tools, or not be ready for them. The tools in the kit are detachable. Use what you can now. This book is a systemic diagnosis and cure, but you do not have to agree with all of it to be part of the solution.

Much of the material in this book is highly condensed, even oversimplified. You cannot skim-read it. Given the interdisciplinary reach of this book, this was necessary in order to make it succinct and widely accessible. I did not want to write a 1200 page-plus tome. I cite or list other sources here, even insisting that you read them in some cases. This will flesh out my material more.

(1) A society characterized by severe and worsening inequality, fear, greed, economic crisis, declining quality of life for most people, a swarm of serious chronic diseases and social pathologies, relentless degradation of the biosphere human life depends on, and most fundamentally, the lack of a real spiritual foundation in people's lives, cannot be characterized as "well".

Introduction/about the author

I'm a self-educated redneck, being up to 75% Scots-Irish. Ancestry in America going back to 1700. Ancestors, the Younger brothers, who ran with Jesse James. That makes me what U.S. cultural right-wingers call a "Real American", a stupid phrase, since only "Indians", more so "wild Indians", are Real Americans.

Like most redneck boys, my Dad gave me plenty of exposure to the back woods, from the time I was three. In the 4th grade, my teacher, who I loved (a closet hippie, this was during the fall of 1966) presented Ishi, the Last of His Tribe, to the class with great enthusiasm (Ishi was the last surviving "wild Indian" in the U.S.A.). Only me and my two best buddies, Kenny and Dave, got it. Some of the other kids called Ishi "icky Ishi". This was in a multi-racial urban working-class neighborhood in the (S.F. area) East Bay.

I've always wanted to return to the Wild, I just never thought it realistic. The more I learn, the more I know this isn't true – at least for the first pioneers at this time.

Much later, in 2000, being a radical, I happened upon an article written by John Zerzan, titled No Way Out? The lights went on. Already long committed to the emancipation of working people (starting with myself), I was a green anarchist waiting to happen.

To git ideological and all, this book is a beginning attempt to fuse class-war libertarianism (we live in a class war) with green libertarianism (we live on/from the Land). In America, the word "libertarian" has been ripped-off by well-heeled capitalists and their supporters ("Social Darwinists", and later, Ayn Rand sociopaths) from the original libertarian wing of the working class/labor movement. (Capitalists are thieves. Surprise. Surprise.) We need to take it back.

A historical note here. Redneck is the part of the U.S. working-class with a Scots-Irish core. The founding core of our working-class, before

1776, included 400,000 Scots-Irish settlers, 300,000 British indentured servants (who fled West and were absorbed by the Scots-Irish), and 300,000 African slaves. I include here in the term "working class" farmers who are small freeholders, as well as tenant farmers and sharecroppers.

My extended biological family (I won't say more here, not to bad-mouth them) are social-climbers who were quick to shed their redneck roots. I'm here to rectify that.

Until recently, I only knew I descended from pioneers/settlers, and that my last name is Scottish. I did not know how my ancestors got here, or what we had been thru before that.

I'd like to credit Born Fighting, by James Webb (he sadly leaves out the admirable history of the United Mine Workers, almost entirely made up of rednecks, who founded the C.I.O.). And the Redneck Manifesto, by Jim Goad, which deals exclusively with the British indentured servant part of the redneck core.

A final personal note. My parents were sympathetic to hippies. I grew up on the Doors and the Hair album (as well as cowboy ballads). Initially revolted by hippies "they're weird", I remember seeing lurid TV accounts of bad trips on LSD. "**Why** do people take that stuff?!" My Mom said: "some people have had wonderful experiences on it".

My Dad's cousin had. I remember my Mom's hope in the 1960's. She was afraid to take the plunge (she had kids). But when it was time, I did. 40 times, at doses of up to 600 mcg..

"That Hair album **made** me take all that **terrible** LSD." For which I'm immensely grateful. I was allowed to play in the fields of God(*) for a year. Then that **nasty** LSD began bringing up the difficult stuff. But I knew – I'm going to see all this after I die, then it will be too late to do anything about it. I had a 3-layer character disorder. Sort of like a wedding cake, except that the layers are all kind of smushed into each other, making what is really going on difficult to git. Welcome to the world of Fallen humans.

It should be noted that Jim Morrison and Janis Joplin also descended from rednecks. Too bad they never found God. They would not have died so young.

One last note here. One of the most pernicious lies around is that only a special, esoteric, highly evolved elite get to have what has been called mystical experience. If the level of experience I was given, many times, could be given to someone as damaged as I was, **it could be given to any of us.** In fact, this is exactly the intent of Reality.

(*) God: The inmost, final Reality all creation emanates from.

One of the things my parents did right is that they did not shove religion down my throat as a kid. So when the time came, I was able to approach God with a completely open heart and mind – unobstructed by idolatrous preconceptions and other baggage. I will not belabor the monstrous historical crimes of the Church, many of them genocidal in scale. Jesus put it well concerning the religious "authorities" of his time: You have shut the kingdom of God in the face of mankind.

A must-read footnote to my Eden chapter bears repeating here:

6. "God" for all too many people quickly becomes a gigantic ego or superego (parent or cop) in the sky. This is idolatry, and probably the biggest reason Buddhism insists that there is no God at all.

It is not possible to directly encounter the incomprehensibly deep love Reality has for us without being overcome with gratitude and reverence. But this is not because God has any need to be worshipped. Nor does Reality have any selfish ends or any need to control us. God has no self as we are even remotely capable of comprehending it. Nor can there ever be any such thing as "my" God – like that spiritually ignorant, idolatrous U.S. officer in Iraq who said "My God is bigger than your God".

"The description of God by means of negations is the correct description – a description that is not affected by an indulgence in facile language . . . With every increase in the negations regarding God, you come nearer to the apprehension of God." (Moses Maimonides, Guide of the Perplexed, 1: 58-59)

God is in fact not describable, and we slide towards idolatry even attempting to do so.

The Return

A LETTER OF SOLIDARITY
FROM REDPANTHER
Re: Segorea Te/Glen Cove Native American occupation

The entire Earth is being desecrated.

The children of the invaders don't know how to live here. To a sad degree, they don't know how to live at all.

Your recent ancestors had this Knowledge, and you retain, to various degrees, much of it, despite vicious, prolonged attempts by the invaders to destroy it. How we were intended to live has been called the Way. It is my understanding that the full recovery of the Way is the most fundamental task of Native Americans and your allies. This recovery, and the return to the Land, I have called the Return. What is at stake here? Nothing less than the redemption of all humans.

This will require the repatriation of serious amounts of Land to the descendants of the Original People ("Indians") who know how to live here. In Northern and Central California, serious would start with thousands of square miles, and in appropriate time, expand to at least 30,000 square miles.

Nearly all "white" people own **no** Land or only a pitiful debt-loaded (and often underwater) crumb. **Who** can live decently on a tiny city lot? Humans need wild space to be happy.

(People of European decent only have a sickly whitish pallor when imprisoned in office cubicles or factories. We are normally, when free to live like normal humans, a tawny color, like a cougar, only more red.)

Nearly all U.S. Land in the West is owned by logging corporations, large agribusiness, railroads, utilities, and mining corporations – all almost totally owned by the richest 1% of the U.S. population, wealthy individuals,

1

and the (capitalist) State – which allows logging corporations to rape the "public" forest – to build 3000 sq. ft. yuppie houses (and even **bigger** McMansions.) Aren't we blessed?!

Your stolen Land is held by a **class** enemy, not a racial one. And only working people as a whole have the (potential) power to destroy capitalist rule.

Gray Eagle said to me, about his People "we were defeated". Not long from now, those who have bought in to the spiritually dead, greedily depraved attitude about life that is capitalism will be staring defeat in the face. This has already started. Aside from the severe structural economic problems of an (inherently) sick/depraved system, consider, for starters:

1. The degenerate way of "life" that the invaders brought here breeds a host of plagues and diseases, most of which are incurable – which will in time create a health-care mess that by itself will take down the whole economy.
2. In as little as 100 years, many of the invader's cities will be underwater.
3. Industrial civilization is unsustainable.

Not long from now, the children of the invaders will **have** to learn the Way. There will be no choice.

The Way we were intended to live is literally encoded in our DNA. I call this the Biological Torah. This Deep Structure has to be enabled by phase-appropriate formative experience growing up. Genes are enabled by formative **experience**. With the destruction of the Way, our young are not getting this, and so end up with a damaged/deformed Deep Structure. And all the resulting problems.

Damaged, but not destroyed. The Land emanates directly from Reality (God), and through this Emanation, Reality will teach even the children of the invaders directly if we open ourselves deeply enough.

Working people as a whole will need to understand all this, given what is going to come down.

My war name is Redpanther.
My tribe is Scots-Irish/redneck

If you happen to know rednecks who are Native American friendly – please pass this on. My tribe needs to git ready for the class war.

On "primitivism"*, or
Why the human memory of Eden won't go away

*(The word 'primitive' has been applied to people who lived before class society, based on their technology. When applied to mental and even physical health, this word becomes a problem. These people were healthy and we are degenerate.

Those who are appalled by this assertion may want to check out the tasteful, social-democratic version of primitivism, which is called Evolutionary Psychology. It even got a cover article in Time magazine – a noted organ of anarchist propaganda – titled The Evolution of Despair, 8-28-95.)

The paleoanthropologists of our time have been dazed and confused (for so long it's not true) by the huge brains of our ancient ancestors (by ancient I mean 50,000 to 800,000 years back) (7), given their apparent lack of what we call art. And from this we surmise a lack of symbol formation (language) as we know it – words, grammar, and syntax like we have now.

Yet their stone tools were finely made – probably in what we would call a meditative state – and are much more beautiful than they needed to be merely to function (see plate 1 - 500,000 years old).

"If these people didn't have language like we do, what were they doing with these huge brains?"

Seeing God.

Religion (and the inherently idolatrous **abstraction** of God) is the largely co-opted and rotted hulk of symbol-formation around what was originally, before the Biblical Fall of humanity, a direct, unmediated relationship with Reality (6).

Anyone who has been given Direct Knowledge understands directly how crude and shallow language is. And how crude and shallow even our finest art is compared to wild nature itself.

Symbol-formation, like the information technology based on it, is more efficient than direct or intuitive forms of knowledge at certain limited tasks. As pointed out by John Zerzan (in his "extremist" critique of language and art) – when words and "virtual reality" overrun directly lived reality (the disease of late Homo sapiens) – we have problems.

It is no coincidence that spiritual practice attempts to still this endless diarrhea of symbol-formation, not by moralistically trying to stifle it (and becoming attached to this campaign of stifling), but by letting go of it, so that in time we begin to have direct, unmediated experience.

Or what was **normal** for our non-degenerate ancestors.

". . . to say we wouldn't want to live in our primitive past isn't to say we can't learn from it. It is, after all, the world in which our currently malfunctioning minds were designed to work like a Swiss watch." (Evolution of Despair, Time, 8-28-95, pg. 52)

A Swiss watch is a very, very crude analogy.

The minds of our ancient ancestors were organized very differently than ours today. Direct Knowledge is called 'mysticism' because it is mysterious to those who (in our degenerate condition) have never had this level of experience. And because those who have **cannot** reduce it to symbol-formation, and because the intellect **cannot** grasp it. The best of the Scriptures can only give clues, and these remnant clues use symbol-formation sparingly.

Our ancestors saw God every day.

We saw each other and the rest of wild nature (from which we had no separation) directly as we emanate from this inmost, final Reality.

(A fragmented or poorly translated remnant of this is the "primitive" experience or intuition that trees, animals, and rocks have spirits in them.) And so we were uninterested in the fallen things of class society. (5)

The Deep Structure of human nature (the "Swiss watch" referred to in Time) was able to unfold mostly intact (unlike today) because we had the formative experiences that enable this unfolding.

At the most material level, these experiences "switch on" the thousands of genes (**many** during critical effect periods) that enable the vastly complex interrelated neural structures of the Deep Structure to form. Genes are activated by **experience**. (1)

This was the biological substrate enabling the "primitive" communism of our ancestors. And for that matter any freely chosen, **actually lived** communism that will ever exist.

The scientists of capitalism, having stumbled upon a materialized pattern in our genome, will attempt to manipulate ("engineer") it to their own ends. They are already trying to map the human brain, and tweak certain genes. Thought control awaits!

It is already apparent that the advanced derangement of everyday life itself is reducing many pieces of the genetic code for the Deep Structure to junk DNA. By adulthood, much of this damage is irreparable, as so many of these genes are very difficult or impossible to "switch on" after their critical effect periods have passed. This is probably the main reason neural plasticity declines so much with age. (See Appendix 2 – Diseases of Late Capitalism. The most documented example of the critical effect period is language itself – kids deprived of human contact till age 5 or 6 never learn how to speak.)

Godless, soulless capitalism cannot grasp the deep, subtle, integrated totality of the Deep Structure; and so Capital will never be able to control it as a **totality**. But Late Capitalist culture has been able to hijack pieces of this Deep Structure, and tweak these pieces into malignant tumors. (Greed – a malignant form of storing food for winter or hard times, and status-seeking – a malignant form of needing to be valued by one's band and tribe – immediately come to mind. These malignancies are driven by the inherent fragmentation and emptiness of Late Capitalist life.)

We are not too far gone yet to be unable to intuit many or even most of the experiences needed to enable the Deep Structure.

Some likely clues:

1. A viable mother-infant bond in the first year of life (including the father and allo-parents). Science already knows (from its own stupid experience) that the **absence** of this **kills** babies – regardless of how warm, dry, well fed, and clean they are kept. (2) This holding environment continues thru the rest of life with the people we are tight with.

2. Genuinely felt encouragement for individuation, starting as early as age 1 – i.e. our kids are distinct individuals with temperaments and lives of their own, **not** appendages of our egos.

3. A warm, close relationship with the same-sex parent, especially between ages 2 and 12, and with other kids of our own sex between age 5 and 12. (3)

4. Immersion in wild nature, and from this seeing our belonging to it, starting at age 1.

5. Lots of opportunity for play, starting before age 1. (4)

6. Successful resolution of the "Oedipus Complex" (gender/sexual formation), around age 4-6.

7. Stable belonging to a single extended family (band) – based on both blood and blood-joining (buddies for life), most critically throughout childhood, but also throughout life.

8. Stable belonging to a single neighborhood or workplace (remnant analogue to tribe or People; class – as in working class, or nationality are extensions of this).

9. Just as ethics are taught by **example**, so a healthy spiritual life will tend to grow spontaneously out of the opportunities for healthy development I have mentioned here. Kids will be naturally curious; adolescents and young adults will begin having "mystical experiences" (Direct Knowledge) even **without** psychedelics.

(I suspect our Upper Paleolithic ancestors – 40,000-10,000 years ago – turned to psychedelics and shamen when they were already starting to lose it. Earlier people did not need them. The Fall was a slow, insidious slide towards class society during the Upper Paleolithic, then a complete rupture into it with patriarchy/Neolithic society, not a sudden expulsion from Eden.)

The Deep Structure is inherently natural/anarchist. That is, it will spontaneously self-organize given any opportunity to do so (at least during childhood and adolescence). It **cannot** be intellectually pre-conceived and shoved down people's throats by politically correct planners or cult-like families and churches. The outcomes of these attempts are always deranged and sometimes lethal.

The supremacy of a completely inhuman reality has intuitively gripped the imagination of people living under Late Capitalism – exemplified by the Matrix series. This will be the final stage of class society if it is allowed to fulfill its inherent nature.

Our rulers, and the "gatekeepers" they use to control us, will **not** at their physical core be artificial intelligence or machines. Their physical core will be the DNA of our present capitalist oligarchy, re-engineered, raised in human bodies, and fused with other bioengineering applications, artificial intelligence implants and connections, and nanotechnology applications. Having had human origins at one point, they will no longer be human. (Who but the wealthy are going to start having "designer babies"?)

These rulers will use technology we can scarcely imagine now to enforce their grip on the rest of us. And a world who's natural/biological foundation will be imploding, despite technological attempts to forestall this.

This is the world our children will be left with, should present trends be allowed to continue. And us, for those of us young enough to live another 40 years.

The great human longing for the Mesach (Messiah – Judaism), the Second Coming (Christianity), and the Revolution (anarchism and Marxism) is an unconsciously driven longing for the awakening of the Deep Structure, and the recovery of the direct relationship we once had with Reality.

To paraphrase the first of the Matrix series: The awakening of the Deep Structure, which will herald the destruction of Late Capitalism and all class society.

The Deep Structure is inside each one of us.

Those of us well into adulthood may be irreparably damaged, but our children could be more fortunate. If we wake up, we will intuit what they need (starting with a radically healthier social order). If we are sufficiently open spiritually, we will be shown **directly** how we were intended to live.

And the mind of Reality is **infinite** - unimaginably more intelligent and integrated than any technology the capitalist oligarchy will ever have.

"What makes Mescalito different from an ally?"

"He can't be tamed and used as an ally is tamed and used. Mescalito is outside oneself. He chooses to show himself in many forms to whoever stands in front of him, regardless of whether that person is a brujo or a farm boy."

Don Juan spoke with deep fervor about Mescalito's being the teacher of the proper way to live. I asked him how Mescalito taught the "proper way of life", and Don Juan replied that Mescalito SHOWED how to live.

"How does he show it?" I asked.

"He has many ways of showing it. Sometimes he shows it on his hand, or on the rocks, or the trees, or just in front of you."

"Is it like a picture in front of you?"

"No. It is a teaching in front of you."

"Does Mescalito talk to the person?"

"Yes. But not in words."

"How does he talk, then?"

"He talks differently to every individual."

(from The Teachings of Don Juan, Carlos Castaneda, pg. 52)

Footnotes (must read)

1. NATURE via NURTURE, Matt Ridley, 2003, Harper Collins Publishers.
    You need to read the whole book. Despite the depressing capitalist spin he puts on many of the findings, the shear volume and sweep of research he presents is not to be missed.

    . A GENERAL THEORY of LOVE, T. Lewis, F. Amini, and R. Lannon, 2000, Random House. Human development compared to primate and other mammalian development. Again, you need to read the whole book.

    See also NEURODYNAMICS of PERSONALITY, J. Grigsby, D. Stevens, 2000, The Guilford Press.

2. Study by Rene Spitz, cited in A General Theory of Love (ibid), pg. 69, 70

3. THE TWO SEXES, Eleanor Maccoby, 1998, Harvard University Press
    REAL BOYS, William Pollack, 1998, Random House
    Maccoby, who in the past has tended to see all sex differences in behavior as a result of socialization alone, researches the powerful cross-cultural tendency of boys and girls to spontaneously self-segregate into same-sex play groups/cultures. Attempts to force them into Politically Correct mixed-sex play groups are spontaneously and strongly resisted.

    This powerful tendency is likely the self-organized preparation for belonging to the male and female collectives of adulthood that form the core of the band. Life-long, tight friendships (buddies for life), which will form the core of these collectives in the next generation, are normally formed in childhood.

    The two collectives, and the very different structure of human male and female bodies, are a result of doing very different things – hunting and gathering – for nearly 2 million years.

    At the same time, temperamentally transexed individuals, and temperamentally intersexed (strongly masculine and feminine both) individuals show up in large numbers in both sexes (around 5% and 25% respectively) in all cultures. "Primitive" hunter-gatherer cultures are usually much less hung up about this than "post-modern" Americans. These people mediated between the male and female collectives for hundreds of thousands of years, facilitating their cooperation and the success of their offspring. Which is why "gender transgression" (normal gender variation) became genetically embedded in humans.

4. Team sports (and spontaneously formed analogues) are likely unconscious, symbolic re-enactments of rhinoceros hunts and combat between male groups. They activate many of the same neural predispositions in male humans. Human males have been observed developing an addiction to war (see Chris Hedges two books on war, 2002, 2003). The biggest component of this is the intense bonding among the guys. I suspect these neural predispositions are the result of hundreds of thousands of years of collectively hunting big game. Taking on rhinos or cave bears, or fighting off/killing saber-toothed tigers is violent, high-risk behavior requiring tight teamwork. And it had to be done repeatedly. Our "addiction" to this Politically Incorrect behavior enabled us to provide for and defend each other and our bands.

5. Science has even discovered areas in the brain, in the temporal lobes, that when electrically stimulated induce a powerful state of transcendence in people who had no conscious spiritual or religious beliefs. These areas of the brain were well developed in Homo erectus, Homo heidelbergensis, Homo neandertalis, as well as our species, Homo sapiens.

    (Neuroscientist Michael Persinger, Laurentian University, Canada, 1995, and neurologists at U.C. San Diego, quoted in Mapping the Mind, Rita Carter, 1998, University of California Press, pg. 13, 19.)

    Studies also show a big spike in oxytocin activity in individuals who have entered a mystical state (see MAPS website).

    This will no doubt appall Religion, like LSD did ("God in a Pill?!"). But here even Godless science has shown that we are physically hard-wired for a direct relationship with the final Reality that all creation emanates from.

12

6. "God" for all too many people quickly becomes a gigantic ego or superego (cop or parent) in the sky. This is idolatry, and probably the biggest reason Buddhism insists that there is no God at all.

It is not possible to directly encounter the incomprehensibly deep love Reality has for us without being overcome with gratitude and reverence. But this is not because God has any need to be worshipped. Nor does Reality have any selfish ends or any need to control us. God has no self as we are even remotely capable of comprehending it. Nor can there ever be any such thing as "my" God – like that spiritually ignorant, idolatrous U.S. officer in Iraq who said "my God is bigger than your God".

"The description of God by means of negations is the correct description – a description that is not affected by an indulgence in facile language . . . With every increase in the negations regarding God, you come nearer to the apprehension of God." (Moses Maimonides, Guide of the Perplexed, 1: 58-59)

God is in fact not describable, and we slide towards idolatry even attempting to do so.

Those religious laws that actually WERE inspired by Direct Knowledge were intended for OUR benefit, not any sick need on the part of God to control us and make us miserable. Shabbat is one of the most obvious examples. Try going without a day of rest each week and see what happens! Even the prohibition on promiscuity, considered oppressive by those wallowing in Late Capitalist decay, was intended for our benefit. Aside from the dubious benefit of treating other people (and oneself) like pieces of meat, promiscuity, when people have been herded into cities, is a highly efficient vector for spreading plagues – as the present AIDS epidemic makes all too clear. People already lived in cities (some huge – like Rome with 1 million inhabitants) when the Bible was written.

7. CRANIAL CAPACITY OF HUMAN FOSSIL SPECIMENS

Specimen	Age	Cranial Capacity	Species
Sangrian 17	800,000 years old	1029 c.c.	Homo erectus
Peking Man	500,000 " "	1043 c.c.	H. erectus
Petralonia 1	400,000	1220 c.c.	H. heidelbergensis

Arago 2	400,000	1160 c.c.	"
Atapuerca 5	300,000	1390 c.c.	"
Broken Hill 1	300,000	1300 c.c.	"
Omo 2	195,000	1435 c.c.	"
Idaltu	154,000	1450 c.c.	H. sapiens
Qafzeh 9	100,000	1554 c.c.	"
Skhul 5	90,000	1518 c.c.	H. sapiens /neandertalis
La Ferrassie 1	50,000	1620 c.c.	H. neandertalis
Amud 1	45,000	1740 c.c.	H. sapiens/neandertalis
Cro-Magnon 1	32,000	1600 c.c.	H. sapiens

(all from Lucy to Language, by Donald Johanson and Blake Edgar, 1996 – except Omo 2, Nature, 2-17-05)

Modern H. sapiens average 1375 c.c. (comparison of H. sapiens idaltu with 3000 contemporary males, S.F. Chronicle, 6-12-03).

Smaller brains, plus smaller, weaker skeletons with rotting teeth are hard evidence of mental and physical degeneration since the emergence of class society 10,000 years ago.

APPENDIX 1

Exodus 10:4

Thou shalt not make unto thee a graven image, nor any manner of likeness, of anything that is in heaven above, or that is in the earth beneath, or that is in the water under the earth.

Plate 1. NOT IDOLATRY

Late Acheulean tools, 500,000 years old

Plate 2. TRANSITIONAL TO IDOLATRY

Contemporary drawing done by author in a psychedelic state (psilocybin), similar to Upper Paleolithic cave paintings. (I was immersed in wild nature as a kid.)

Below: IDOLATRY

"In the beginning was the Word, and the Word was with God, AND THE WORD WAS GOD."

(John 1:1, emphasis added)

APPENDIX 2:
The diseases of Late Capitalism.

(WARNING: This is the most depressing section of the book, isolated in an appendix that can be passed over until you have the stomach for it. It isn't enough to just say "this is a sick society". The evidence has to be presented.)

NOTES ON MY UNFINISHED RESEARCH

I don't have trend data for drug addiction (including smoking and Rush Limbaugh's pills), but I think these have only gone up moderately in the last 20 years, after a big rise from 1950 to 1980 (continuing thru 1985 for cocaine and crack).

No figures for anorexia & bulimia, or promiscuity and hyperpromiscuity, which I think will show exponential growth. None for rape, wife-beating, or child-molesting and other child abuse – all of which are as old as patriarchy. None for "workaholism", greed (compulsive wealth hoarding), "shopaholics", obsessive-compulsive disorders (OCD), or TV addicts.

All of these are gross (measurable) manifestations of the fragmentation and emptiness of Late Capitalist life, described well by Guy Debord and Christopher Lasch. The underlying character structures Late Capitalism tends to produce – the narcissistic and borderline personalities being the most common – are hard to quantify.

The inherent nature of the culture/economy we live in is driving most of the chronic, debilitating physical illnesses – such as cancer, heart disease, diabetes, strokes, liver disease, HIV/AIDS - that drive endlessly ballooning health care costs.

There is a second huge factor, separate from this, that drives a monstrosity swallowing just under 20% of the U.S. economy (as of 2012, **twice** the share in any other "developed" country, and growing every year). That is the U.S. Healthcare Fraud and Extortion Racket itself. I call it that because that is exactly what it is. You **must** read the Time magazine expose, 3-4-13, to see how it operates – see also my very brief summary of this in chapter 9 of this book. The biggest reason preventative care/education has been neglected is that there is far too little $$$ in it. It is far more lucrative to viciously gouge people when they get seriously ill (usually chronically).

As a Brazilian anarchist put it: "major structural reforms are more utopian than a social revolution" (Anarchy #54, pg. 8)

CHRONIC SERIOUS DISEASE OVERVIEW

". . . 'the trajectory we are on is unsustainable.' The study looked at seven of the most costly chronic illnesses: the most common forms of cancer, hypertension, mental disorders, heart disease, diabetes, pulmonary conditions such as asthma, and stroke.

'More than half of Americans suffer from chronic disease. Every year, millions of people are diagnosed, and every year millions die of these diseases.' (numbers exclude people in institutions such as nursing homes and prisons). (The Milken Institute's "Unhealthy America: The Economic Burden of Chronic Disease", reported in S.F. Chronicle, 10-3-07)

ERODING SOCIAL TRUST

"As of 1993, 37% of Americans felt they could trust most people, down from 58% in 1960." (Time, Evolution of Despair, 8-28-95) "In a Pew Research survey from Apr. 2012 . . . only 29% of people age 18-29 said most people could be trusted, vs. 37% of all respondents." (Pew Research, 5-23-13) So much for "idealistic youth". As everyone knows, the young are by far the most addicted to a "virtual social life" (see sub-appendix: "Just for u", Techie addiction and the galloping social rot of Late Capitalism)

SLEEP DEPRIVATION

Nearly one-third of American workers get 6 hours of sleep a night or less (CDC, cited in the Economist, 8-17-13, pg.58). In 1960, only 2% of

American adults got 7 hours of sleep or less each night (N.Y. Times, 4-28-13). Sleep deprivation is used by cults, and causes brain damage in children.

DEPRESSION

"Among women born around the time of World War 1, only 1% had experienced serious depression at some point in their lives. For those born around the time of World War 2, the percentage was 3%. Among those born around the time of the Korean War, 7%. For those born during the Viet Nam era, 10%. And among those born in the post-Viet Nam era, between 12% and 15% had had a serious episode of depression by the time they had completed high school." (NIMH study quoted by William Mattox Jr. in the S.F. Chronicle, 4-8-99)

"Over the past decade, scientists have discovered that depression, which plagues millions, recurs repeatedly in 4 out of 5 patients." "A comprehensive review of 30 years of evidence, published this week in the Lancet medical journal . . . " (S.F. Chronicle, 2-21-03)

". . . a study published in today's Archives of Internal Medicine found that . . . depressed women faced a 73% higher heart disease risk than non-depressed women, but they were not at greater risk of dying. Men with depression had a 71% higher heart disease risk, and were 2.34 times more likely to die of heart disease than non-depressed men." (quoted in S.F. Chronicle, 5-8-00)

"The nation's teenage suicide rate has tripled in 20 years, and is the third-leading cause of death in that age group, after accidents and homicides, according to the federal Centers for Disease Control and Prevention." (S.F. Chronicle, 8-26-99) It should be noted here that a lot of accidents and homicides are a result of people putting themselves in situations (often unconsciously) where they can be suicided.

ANXIETY/STRESS and RESULTING DISEASES

"When researchers examined rural villagers in Samoa, they discovered what were by Western standards extraordinarily low levels of cortisol, a biochemical by-product of anxiety. And when a Western anthropologist tried to study depression among the Kaluli of New Guinea, he couldn't find any." (from The Evolution of Despair, Time, 8-28-95)

"All had blood pressure levels considered pre-hypertensive or Stage 1 high blood pressure – **levels shared by more than half of Americans**. Their systolic blood pressure ... was in the range of 120 to 159 ... Their diastolic readings ... 80 to 99." (Journal of the American Medical Association, quoted in the Washington Post, 11-16-05; emphasis added – presumably this refers to adult Americans.)

Back surgery:	1993	2001	
Vertebra trimming	425,000	635,000	
Spinal fusion	160,000	325,000	(Newsweek, 4-26-04, pg.47)

"In the HIZ study, the best predictor of pain was not how bad the defect looked but the patient's level of psychological distress." (ibid., pg. 45)

"Studies have shown that drinking excessively – 5 or more drinks daily – can increase the risk of heart disease. The Centers for Disease Control says nearly 1 in 3 Americans drinks too much." (CDC study published in the May issue of the American Journal of Preventative Medicine, quoted in the S.F. Chronicle, 4-19-05)

"From 1985 to 1992, the costs of alcoholism and alcohol-related problems rose by more than 40% to $148 billion, according to the National Institutes of Health." (S.F. Chronicle, 1-27-04)

"When exposed to mild stress induced in a laboratory setting, women in the study who suffered from depression and had a history of childhood abuse showed levels of ACTH, a hormone secreted by the pituitary gland in response to stress, 6 TIMES as high as those women in the study without such histories." "the study, which appears in today's issue of the Journal of the AMA" (S.F. Chronicle, 8-2-00)

OTHER AFFLICTIONS

"If the separation is prolonged, a mammal enters the second stage: despair. Like protest, despair is a coherent physiologic state – a set of behavioral inclinations and bodily reactions common to mammals." "Despair and depression are close cousins, enough so that despair in laboratory animals is often used as a model for human depressive illness." ". . . cardiovascular function, hormone levels, and immune processes are all disturbed in adults subjected to prolonged separation."

"dozens of studies demonstrate that solitary people have a vastly increased rate of premature death from all causes . . . " (from A General Theory of Love; Lewis, Amini, & Lannon 2000 pg. 78-80)

"One out of four students, representing 5.3 million youths, told investigators they had either used a gun or knife, carried such a weapon, or had been involved in an incident in which someone was injured by a weapon in the past year." (Data from National Longitudinal Study of Adolescent Health, analyzed at U. of Minnesota Medical School, quoted in the Washington Post, 11-30-00)

"in a report by the National Marriage Project at Rutgers University that surveyed 21 to 29 year old men and women in five regions. With very slight variations, both sexes had two priorities: gaining financial success and postponing marriage indefinitely." (S.F. Chronicle, 6-12-00)

"One reason the sinews of community are so hard to restore is that they are at odds with free markets. Capitalism not only spews out cars, TVs, and other antisocial technologies; it also sorts people into little vocational boxes and scatters the boxes far and wide." (The Evolution of Despair, Time, 8-28-95)

"In 1995, 18 prominent scientists, including brain, neurological, and behavioral researchers, met in Erice, Sicily, and shared evidence that endocrine-disrupting chemicals, at levels found in the environment and in humans, threaten brain development. In the first months of pregnancy, the developing brain is very sensitive to chemical disruption, and permanent damage can be caused. It shows up as reduced intelligence, learning disabilities, attention-deficit problems, and intolerance to stress – which are not evident when the baby is born." (from The Meaning of the 21st Century, by James Martin, 2007 edition, pg. 171)

OBESITY, STRESS and RESULTING DISEASES

"data released last week by OECD, a Paris-based group of 30 industrialized nations. It found that as obesity in the U.S. has doubled to 26% of the population in the past 20 years, the problem has grown at least as fast in many of its other member countries." (Wall St. Journal, 7-1-02)

"In a separate study, Tufts University researchers found that 63% of men and 55% of women over age 25 are obese or overweight, the highest ever recorded. Obesity leads directly to at least 280,000 deaths every year and perhaps as many as 374,000, according to a new study from St. Luke's/ Roosevelt Hospital Center in N.Y.. That makes obesity the second-leading cause of preventable deaths after smoking . . ." (S.F. Chronicle, 10-27-99)

"In a scant seven years (from 1991 to 1998) we had a 50% increase in obesity in all age groups and in all ethnic groups." "The team also found that the incidence of high blood pressure, type 2 diabetes, gall bladder disease, and osteoarthritis increased sharply with increasing obesity." (S.F. Chronicle, 10-27-99)

"Pecoraro and colleagues, led by UCSF physiology Professor Mary D. Dallman, designed a series of experiments in rats to isolate the effects of particular stress hormones maintained for long periods of time at high levels.

Chronic high levels of hormones known as glucocorticoids led to a marked preference for high-fat foods, which over time led to accumulated belly fat. Normally, these fat stores generate a stress-relieving signal in the brain, reducing output of a stress-related chemical called CRF . . ." "But if the stress just doesn't let up, the eating continues – as does the abdominal obesity." (S.F. Chronicle, 9-9-03)

Center for Disease Control: obesity rate is above 40% among baby boomers in Louisiana and Alabama, above 30% in 41 more states. A 2012 CDC projection was a U.S. obesity rate of 42% by 2030, at an annual cost of $500 billion (2012 dollars). CDC projected in 2010 that by 2050, 33% of Americans will be diabetic. (U.S. News, 8-19-13)

"Just 4 u"
Techie addiction and the galloping social rot of Late Capitalism.

In George Orwell's totalitarian nightmare, 1984, the State had invented and imposed a new language – Newspeak – designed to hollow out, flatten, and constrict people's ability to communicate.

Today, never mind the State. The damaged humans of Late Capitalism, especially the young, have invented and imposed Newspeak themselves. We could call it Textspeak. "Texting makes u dumb" as the truism goes. So stop doing it. Except they can't. They're addicted. More learned helplessness, as if we didn't have way too much already.

We are now seeing disturbing results from "virtual reality" addiction. One of the most central trends is declining social trust, which at 29%, has eroded most badly among the age 18-29 set (see main text of this appendix).

The material cited below is from Newsweek, 7-16-12:

"The brains of Internet addicts, it turns out, look like the brains of alcohol and drug addicts."

". . . other Chinese results that link Internet addiction to 'structural abnormalities in gray matter', namely shrinkage of 10% to 20% in the areas of the brain responsible for processing speech, memory, motor control, emotion, sensory, and other information. And worse, the shrinkage never stopped: the more time online, the more the brain showed signs of atrophy."

"Chinese researchers have similarly found ' a direct effect between heavy Net use and the development of full-blown depression . . ."

From Newsweek, 5-20-13:

From 1966, when the Torrence Tests of Creative Thinking were first administered, through the mid-1980's, creativity scores in children increased. Then they dropped, falling sharply in 1998. Scores on tests of empathy similarly fell sharply, starting in 2000 . . ." " 'People are inflating themselves like balloons on Facebook', says W. Kieth Campbell, a psychology professor at the U of Georgia, who has written 3 books about intergenerational increases in narcissism . . ."

From Connected Families, "What Is Technology Doing to Us", Lynne Johnson, 7-31-12: " ' Last year, when MTV polled its 13 to 30 year-old viewers on their Web habits, most felt 'defined' by what they put online, 'exhausted' by always having to put it out there, and **utterly unable to look away for fear of missing out.**"

% who check their technologies **every 15 minutes or less:**

Born		Text msg.	Facebook
1990-98	i generation	62%	32%
1980-89	Net Generation	64%	36%
1965-79	Generation X	42%	17%
1946-64	Baby Boomers	18%	8%

(iDisorder, Larry P. Rosen, Ph.D., 2012, 1st chapter)

"In Bakken's general population study (3399 respondents, Norway), based on subject's self-report, 41.4% of Internet 'addicts' reported feelings of depression in the 12-month period prior to the study, compared to 15.8%

of non-problematic users . . . " 36.4% reported anxious feelings vs. 5% of non-problematic users. (Problematic Internet Use: an overview, Elias Aboujaoude, World Psychiatry, June 2010)

Aboujauode, a psychiatrist at the Stanford U School of Medicine, has written a book titled <u>Virtually You: The Dangerous Powers of the E-Personality</u> (2011, W.W. Norton & Co.). The first 10 chapter titles are chilling: E Personality, Delusions of Grandeur, Narcissism, Ordinary Everyday Viciousness, Impulsivity, Infantile Regression and the Tyranny, Love and Sex Recalibrated, The Illusion of Knowledge, Internet Addiction, The End of Privacy.

Also check out <u>iDisorder: Understanding Our Obsession with Technology and Overcoming Its Hold on Us.</u> By Larry D. Rosen, Ph.D. (2012, Macmillan)

From the 1st chapter: "I, along with my colleagues Dr. Nancy Cheever and Dr. L. Mark Carrier, will take you through the more common psychiatric disorders – communication disorders (including aspects of antisocial personality disorder, social phobia, autism and Asperger's syndrome), attention-deficit hyperactivity disorder, depression, obsessive-compulsive disorder, narcissistic personality disorder, hypochondriasis, schizoaffective and schizotypal disorders, body dysmorphia, voyeurism, and addiction – and provide evidence from up-to-date research in a variety of fields ranging from psychology to neuroscience, from sociology to anthropology, from communication to biology, to show how we are all manifesting symptoms of these serious disorders."

Peter Thiel, a tech mogul with a fortune of nearly $2 billion, whines: "I defy you to name one science fiction film – with the possible exception of the Star Trek and Back to the Future series – in which technology is not portrayed as destructive." "The tech industry is an easy scapegoat in this country." (S.F. Chronicle, 2-22-14)

As we can see, a great many of these new technologies are in fact malignant. And because they are so new, we are just beginning to see the results. Never mind the longer standing damage to human brain development caused by pollutants like neurotoxins and endocrine disruptors.

Some will cry: "Nanny-State to the rescue! We need **more** government regulation of people's private lives!" We already have laws against texting while driving, as tens of millions of Americans are so addicted and stupefied by these technologies that they are a danger to themselves and others. A recent study showed that texting while driving is now the leading cause of death among teenagers-exceeding the drunken driving numbers. (S.F. Chronicle, 10/27/14).

It is the inherent nature of capitalism to breed malignant technologies and addictions. More layers of government on top of this mess will not solve the problem. The only cure is the organic regeneration of radically healthier social relations and ways of life.

The health care mess is a very deeply rooted problem that will grow exponentially worse in coming decades (sort of like a malignant tumor). A soulless rat-race society is bearing its fruit.

No one is going to "thrive" until the following are ENDED: the global Race to the Bottom (a.k.a. "globalization" and "free trade"), bone-crushing mortgages, rent gouging, endless crawling commutes every day, pollution and the destruction of the Land, and the "healthcare" racket itself.

Human needs should be provided for by enterprises owned and managed by their workers. Humans need to be living far more intimately with a restored Land, and working fewer hours, not more. A way of life based on fear, greed, and status seeking – a Godless, soulless "life"(despite whatever religious pretense it may have), must be replaced with a real life with a real spiritual foundation.

All of this will require a sustained social upheaval surpassing any in our nation's history.

Green Anarchy on the Silver Screen?!!

Review of Avatar

I have to admit, this movie really moved me, even tho it's a Spectacle (and so **Must** Be Roundly Condemned By All True Anarchists). A Pagan woman, commenting on the movie, said she heard women crying when she went to the restroom at the theatre. I could barely contain myself from crying thru the latter half of the movie. I'm a guy after all, and didn't want to make a public scene. One friend of mine saw the movie 5 times.

Within all but the most severely damaged humans of our time, there is a deep longing for the Return. It is usually unconscious in most people today. The ancient Greeks and Romans had their own story of Eden and our Fall from it. Hinduism posits stages of degeneration. There is immense, largely unconscious grief behind these stories. The Fall **really happened**.

Why was I so moved? I have been given a body of what has been called "mystical experience" (because it is mysterious to those who have not had this level of experience, and **cannot** be explained in words). Rare today, it was **normal** for hunter-gatherer-permaculturist (i.e. normal) humans. I did not need to go to another planet (far less a fantasied place up in the sky called Heaven). It was given to me in the backwoods of Northern California where I grew up. I have been intimate with this Land since I was 3. My Dad took me to the Land I have now when I was 7. I have spent many days in Eden.

For days after I first met God directly, I was speechless. I was able to say one thing: "Everything we have been given is perfect. All the madness that goes on **we create**."

Ewah (which emanates directly from God) is right **here** at home. Ewah here is not dead, and it is capitalist rule that will **die**. Ewah will wipe out the malignancy and restore the Balance. There have been mass extinctions before. As I heard a fundamentalist Christian I grew up with say: God will destroy the destroyers of the Earth. (Revelation 11:18) Ewah will regenerate.

Avatar's biggest flaw, the White Messiah theme (intended to appeal to a predominantly white audience) I think is unintentionally racist. **Most of all – it is just plain impossible**. It would not be possible for a human with a seriously damaged Deep Structure to magically recover all of it in a few months (since so much of this damage is irreparable or very hard to even partially repair), and then go on to lead normal humans, who have completely intact Deep Structures, to victory. The pieces of this fantasy that are plausible are that the insider knowledge and technology transfer (especially **weapons**), that Sully and his buddies brought would be invaluable. And it was said at one point that Sully had a good heart – maybe he was much less damaged than the Late Capitalist degenerates he came to Eden with.

Make **no** mistake. Despite the alien theme, Avatar is all about **humans**. I know enough about hunter-gatherer-permaculturist humans to know that Cameron has done at least some of his homework.

The repeated White Messiah theme draws from a deep wish among the degenerates to magically wipe out our complicity in the extermination of the Original People ("Indians"), and magically recover an intact Deep Structure, enabling our Return to Eden. The **real** Return will be difficult, in stages, require generations, and for most people only undertaken when necessary (by when it may be too late). This difficulty will **require** what has been called "mystical experience" (which I call Direct Knowledge), which Avatar hints at as best as can be done on the silver screen.

National Geographic recently (Dec. 2009) had a good but brief article about the Hadza – a largely intact hunter-gatherer-permaculturist tribe right here on Earth. Their Eden is much harsher and drier than Pandora, but they know how to live well anyway. My commentary:

Is their a global organization or organizations that are working to defend the freedom of the last normal human cultures left alive?

You will notice that the Hadza have had plenty of exposure to civilization/class society, and are really, **really** NOT interested in "living" like that. Their Deep Structure is mostly intact, and they **know** they are free. Slavery isn't life – it is ambulatory **death**.

We do not need to know all the genes of the human Deep Structure (which I also call the Biological Torah) and their vastly complex interrelationships. All we need to know is how to **enable** the Biological Torah with phase-appropriate formative experience. **The Hadza know all this – and they are still alive and free**. They are not a mostly smashed or totally dead culture we only have notes about. We need to know everything about how their young grow up. Also the young of other hunter-gatherer-permaculturist tribes, any we can get reliable information on.

Even the liberals who wrote the National Geographic article get that this isn't just about "saving the savages". The "savages" **will save us**, should we choose to learn from them.

Lastly, we should notice the Right's instinctive **hate** for Avatar. David Brooks, one of the last remaining moderate conservatives, wrote a review of Avatar (for the N.Y. Times) dripping with barely concealed contempt for the attitude about life represented by the Na'vi. It was Brooks who informed me that in 2000, 20% of Americans thought they would be in the top 1% wealth bracket in their lifetime, **and 20% thought they already were**. Talk about mass delusion. (1) And he thought this was a **virtue**.

Hello? Is ANYBODY home? As it has been said: **nature bats last**.

(1) This poll **was** taken at the peak of the NASDAQ bubble. I suspect far fewer people are entertaining these delusions now.

How Normal Human Young Grow Up

The present "human condition" could be described biologically as damaged gene expression (in terms of brain development). This involves extensive epigenetic damage. Epigenetic material sits atop the genes and controls their expression. It is inherited, and changes far more rapidly than core genetic material (the genome itself). Epigenetic material probably has a lot to do with critical effect periods for normal gene expression. Epigenetic damage is reparable in a single lifetime probably to the degree that the critical effect period for the particular genes involved is not rigid. For language as we know it, and very likely the Original Language, it is very rigid.

Some core genetic damage may have occurred as well over the past 10,000 years. This really is irreparable, beyond the issue of critical effect periods for enabling normal gene expression. Until the genetic core of the human Deep Structure is mapped and understood, we will not know this. This will require understanding all the genes involved in normal human brain development, and their interrelationship – like what genes "switch on" what other genes, and what they do. This will require the comparison of normal (hunter-gatherer-permaculturist) human Deep Structure genes with the same genes of the damaged humans who have grown up under Late Capitalism.

How all this pans out in terms of the vastly complex neural architecture of 100 billion brain cells and all their axions (interconnections) is virtually incomprehensible. As one neuroscientist put it: "we do not understand the brain of a fly". We will git a lot of clues though. We already know, for example, about the oxytocin system, which has to do with enabling bonding/love.

We don't need to understand all this anyway. All we need to understand is how normal humans grow up. This is what enables normal human gene expression. Not only are there extensive notes on normal human societies that have been smashed or completely destroyed, there are living hunter-gatherer-permaculturist societies that have been studied. Some, like the poor Hadza, have become major tourist attractions.

Some quotes from two recent books:

THE WORLD UNTIL YESTERDAY Jared Diamond, 2012 Viking/Penguin Group

"Small-scale societies offer us a vast database on child-rearing." (pg. 175) "Studies of modern hunter-gatherers show that an infant is held almost constantly throughout the day, either by the mother or someone else . . . Most hunter-gatherers, especially in mild climates, have constant skin-to-skin contact between the infant and its caregiver. In every known society of human hunter-gatherers and of higher primates, mother and infant sleep immediately nearby . . . . (pg. 184)

A !Kung child begins to separate more frequently from its mother after the age of one and one-half, but those separations are initiated almost entirely by the child itself, inorder to play with other children. (pg. 184)

. . . traditional carrying devices . . . usually place the child vertically upright, facing forwards, and seeing the same world that the care-giver sees. . . . (this) may contribute to !Kung infants being advanced (compared to American infants) in some aspects of neuromotor development. (pg.185)

. . . allo-parenting is much more important, and parents play a less dominant role, in traditional societies. In hunter-gatherer bands, the allo-parenting begins within the first hour after birth. Newborn Aka and Efe infants are passed from hand to hand around the campfire, from one adult or older child to another, to be kissed, bounced, and sung to and spoken to in words they cannot possibly understand. (pg.187)

The allo-parents are materially important as additional providers of food and protection . . . But allo-parents are also psychologically important, as additional social influences and models beyond the parents themselves. Anthropologists working with small-scale societies often comment on what strikes them as the precocious development of social skills among children in those societies . . . (pg. 189, 190)

. . . observers of children in hunter-gatherer societies commonly report that, if an infant begins crying, the parent's practice is to respond immediately . . . many responses are by non-mothers (especially other adult women) who react by touching or holding the infant. The result is that !Kung infants spend at most one minute out of each hour crying, mainly in crying bouts of less than 10 seconds. (pg.191-192)

Similarly, in modern Africa, the Aka pygmies never beat or even scold their children, and they consider horrible and abusive the child-rearing practices of the neighboring Ngandu farmers, who do beat their children. (pg. 193)

At the risk of overgeneralizing, one could say that hunter-gatherers are fiercely egalitarian, and that they don't tell anyone, not even a child, to do anything. . . . That theme of autonomy has been emphasized by observers of many hunter-gatherer societies. For example, Aka pygmy children have access to the same resources as adults . . . Among the Martu people of the Western Australian desert, the worst offense is to impose on a child's will, even if the child is only 3 years old. ". . . This style of parenting has the result of producing very tough and resilient adults who do not believe that anyone owes them anything" (Daniel Everett) (pg.197)

"The Pirahas' view that children are equal citizens of society means that there is no prohibition that applies to children but does not equally apply to adults and vice versa . . . They have to decide for themselves to do or not to do what society expects of them. Eventually they learn that it is in their best interests to listen to their parents a bit." (Daniel Everett) (pg. 197)

The young children gain from being socialized not only by adults but also by older children. That experience gained by older children contributes to explaining how hunter-gatherers can become confident parents already as teen-agers. (pg. 201)

. . . education in small-scale societies is not a separate activity. Instead, children learn in the course of accompanying their parents and other adults, and hearing stories told by adults and older children around the campfire. (pg. 205)

". . . at age 6, Nakaya children independently go hunting small game, visiting and staying with other families, free from supervision by their own specific parents, though not necessarily from adults . . ." (Nurit Bird-David) (pg. 205)

". . . one day they find that the games they have been playing are not games any longer, but the real thing, for they have become adults. . . . It happens so gradually that they hardly notice the change at first, for even when they are proud and famous hunters their life is still full of fun and laughter." (Colin Turnbull) (pg. 205, 206)

A recurring theme is that other Westerners and I are struck by the emotional security, self-confidence, curiosity, and autonomy of members of small-scale societies, not only as adults, but already as children. We see that people in small-scale societies spend far more time talking to each other than we do, and they spend no time at all on passive entertainment supplied by outsiders, such as TV, video games, and books. We are struck by the precocious development of social skills in their children. (pg. 208)

THE HADZA Frank Marlowe 2010 University of California Press

Obst, a German, described the Hadza as doting parents (compared to the neighboring Bantu, ed. – farmers, pastoralists), saying "I never saw in this region such concerned mothers or active family fathers . . ." . . . Another German observer, Kohl-Larsen (1958), said children were not punished. (pg. 196)

Hadza children are allowed to do as they like most of the time. . . . During one year . . . I saw only one spanking. (pg. 197) Children go from being extremely spoiled during their "terrible twos and threes" to being perfectly well-behaved and respectful of adults – even obedient little servants – by the time they are 4 or 5 years old. . . . Adults express no sex preference and welcome a male or female baby equally. Both sexes are reared with equally little discipline. (pg. 198)

. . . there is not much difference in the way adults treat boys and girls. Differences in behavior begin to emerge nonetheless. For example, while 3 or 4 years old, boys and girls often play together; by age 6 or 7, they more often play in same-sex groups. By age 8 to 10, boys go foraging or play with other boys, while girls begin to go foraging with their mothers. (pg. 199)

Hadza children over 3 or 4 years of age are looked after by the older children they are playing with, though it is still necessary that some adult be within earshot . . . Toddlers are almost never left in camp without an adult or teenager there, but this can be almost anyone. . . . Despite a willingness to leave children with others, Hadza mothers provide the bulk of direct care. Men are affectionate with children and play with them more than women do. (pg.200) Men often babysit toddlers who are left in camp while the women are foraging. (pg. 206)

The Formation of Humankind

When the first upright-walking apes split off from the common ancestor with the chimpanzees – between 6 and 7 million years ago, the culture that emerged was less human than the chimps. The males became half-again the size of females – the same size difference found in baboons. (Chimpanzee males are only 20% bigger than females – much like humans, and in the closely related bonobos, the sexes are equal in size.)

Baboons were the only large primates besides upright apes adapted to the east African woodlands and savannah.

Baboon culture is a vicious patriarchy. It is ordinary for males to dismember and kill over dominance, and the dominant male in the troop gets all the females. They are appropriated as a harem, being yanked or bitten (baboons have fangs) if they stray too far from their owner's reach. (1)

Between 3 and 2 million years ago, the earth's climate underwent a major cooling. This dried the east African habitat of the upright apes – meaning much less woodland and a lot more savannah. This prodded a number of divergent evolutionary adaptions.

At least two species emerged with massive jaws and molars to process large amounts of lower-quality plant food. These jaws and the huge gut needed to digest this food precluded much growth in brain size.

Around 2.5 million years ago, the mutation of a gene that codes for a protein called myosin crippled the ability of some upright apes to develop huge jaw muscles. This both forced a reliance on higher quality food - in a savannah environment this meant meat, and allowed more room for brain growth. (2) This was the beginning of our genus – Homo.

Early species of Homo depended on scavenging (and the first crude meat-cutting tools show up). This required the males to fight off packs of hyenas, with clubs and rocks, a difficult task since early Homo males were considerably smaller than Homo sapien males. This could only be done by a tightly organized **collective** of males. Proto-human males could not yet hunt big game in groups, and **no** alpha male could possibly do this alone, or take from a weaker male who hunted alone, like chimps do. (Chimp troops also divide up their foraging areas, high ranking females getting the best parts.) (3)

This opened up an unprecedented opportunity. The males could use their new collective power to kill the alpha male – ridding themselves of a much worse baboon-like oppressor.

Repeated attempts became more effective over time. This was jail-break time for the female harem (the average female being only one-half the size of the alpha male, it is highly unlikely that the females could have taken on and killed him). And the meat was more equally divided, strengthening the collective and its reproductive success (5). Male reproductive success now became dependent on tight bonding with other males and winning over a female, since females could now **choose** their mates.

Our genus, our kind, was born in bloody revolution – repeated over and over until it changed our bodies as well as our psychic/neural Deep Structure into something human. This is embedded in our collective unconscious – a likely source of Freud's theory of the primal horde killing and eating the autocratic alpha male. And the persistent human capacity to destroy an oppressor rather than grovel before it.

The most successful species emerging out of this process, around 1.8 million years ago – early Homo erectus (now sometimes called Homo ergaster) – had a fully human body (4), a brain starting at twice the size of the upright apes, and radically less size difference between males and females. This indicates, along with more developed tool making and a hunter-gatherer economy, a radically different culture. The first culture that could be called human.

Homo erectus was an accomplished hunter. Meat eating fed brain growth driven by the concurrent need for more advanced levels of cooperation, tool making, and an extended family structure unprecedented in any other species.

Terrence Deacon, in The Symbolic Species (1997), lays out some of the core structural features of this human family:

"reliance on resources relatively unavailable to females with small children selects not only for cooperation between the father and the mother, but for cooperation of relatives and friends." (pg.387) Ed. – particularly among the guys who hunt collectively.

"What is common to all [human societies] is something that is exceedingly rare in other species: cooperative, mixed-sex social groups with significant male care and provisioning of offspring." (pg. 388)

"Group living and male provisioning can occur together only in instances where reproductive access is completely limited and unambiguous, as in the case of social carnivores." ". . . almost all human societies, beginning probably with Homo habilis and Homo erectus, are exceptions to the general rule." (pg. 392)

Deacon sees this extended family as a "highly volatile social structure, highly susceptible to disintegration", in large part because a male's "time and energy will benefit the genes of another male" (pg.388)

Reciprocal altruism overcame this, deeply enough to allow this new "unstable" family structure to endure for nearly 2 million years. Deacon notes that "reciprocal altruism is found in other species, though it does not appear to be generally widespread". (pg.398)

Biologists and paleoanthropologists are (unconsciously) influenced by Late Capitalist culture – with its nuclear families (themselves a disintegration product) eroding into the final stage of social decay: sexual "scenes". And so they assume that **individual** reproductive success, even at the degenerate level of "scoring"/"hookups", motivates human behavior. The viable upbringing of human young **requires** a prolonged investment of energy and resources from **both** parents and the whole human band. Humans are a striking example of **group** rather than individual natural selection. Reciprocal altruism is the behavioral foundation of Paleolithic communism.

For close to 2 million years – 400 times the entire length of recorded history – human reproductive success was inherently collectivized. Particularly among males, who, lacking claws and fangs, had to hunt collectively, in an organized way with weapons, to provide for our young. And in hunting very big game (we took down rhinoceroses 500,000 years ago) we had to risk our lives for each other.

Deacon theorizes that marking off reproductive access with marriage made this possible, ignoring the fact that most known hunter-gatherer cultures are non-monogamous (see R. Leaky, People of the Lake, pg. 99, 100).

It took more than marking off females – the guys had to love each other. A guy had to so love his buddies, whom he had been tight with since he was 5 or 6, that he would provide for their kids as if they were his own flesh and blood. This is why guys join blood.

Blood-joining is a massively cross-cultural male rite, an archetype, despite long-standing attempts by the Church to wipe it out (they felt it trivialized the Eucharist).

It is a gut thing, pre-dating language as we know it, probably going all the way back to the formation of Homo erectus.

The hunter-gatherer culture is an alliance of two separate cultures/ economies. In Neanderthal cultures, men and women had separate camps. Among Ishi's people, the Yahi, men and women spoke separate dialects (Ishi was the last "wild Indian" in California). A guy spent most of his time with his buddies (and sons after they were 5 or so, who also hung out with each other when their dads were off hunting).

None of this resulted in patriarchy. Women had chosen their husbands since the destruction of the upright-ape baboon-patriarchy. And women were too busy with their own culture to predicate their happiness on keeping a man.

Except in boreal climates, women brought in 60% - 70% of the food, plus medicinal plants. The female collective could withhold food from any male who abused his wife or kids.

Women also carried weapons, as they had to protect their kids and each other from predators when the men were off hunting. This need was a powerful evolutionary force selecting for larger females – reducing the size difference from the 1.5 – 1 level of the upright apes down to the level found in Homo erectus and modern humans.

Normal (hunter-gatherer-permaculturist) human societies do not tolerate persistently antisocial behavior – such as rape or wife-beating, child abuse/molestation, attempts to manipulate/exploit others, freeloading (a form of exploitation), or bullying. Persistent perpetrators of this kind of behavior are rare in normal human societies – less than 1% of the population, and almost always the result of serious genetic deformity, as all young have every opportunity to grow up healthy. Persistently antisocial individuals are expelled from the tribe and not allowed to reproduce – keeping the gene pool clean. In severe cases, they are put to death. (6)

Anthropologist Phillip Walker has studied the bones of over 5000 children from hundreds of pre-industrial cultures. He has yet to find the scattered bone bruises that are the skeletal hallmark of the battered child syndrome. (Time, 8-28-95, pg.53)

Our deep and genetically embedded need for the trusting, life-long relationships of early communism, and our collective (usually unconscious) memory of this experience, is the source of the Eden story in the Bible.

And the continuing failure of capitalism to get a totalitarian grip on the world, despite all the resources at its command, and all the wishful thinking summed up in TINA ("There Is No Alternative").

(A note on sources. I have not footnoted the known outlines of human evolution I lay out here, except below. This would take up to 20 footnotes with 3 to 15 citations each. The material here is summarized from the bibliography attached at the end of this chapter. My theory on the destruction of the upright-ape (Australopithecene) patriarchy is stated as fact. It does fit everything we know about the transition from the apiths to Homo erectus. This theory was also prefigured by Freud's theory of the primal horde killing the alpha male, which I consider an intuition from the human collective unconscious (Jung), or what I call species-memory.)

footnotes

1. S.F. Chronicle, science section, 2-26-01

2. Nature, 3-25-04

3. National Geographic, 4-03

4. Early Homo erectus had a smaller opening in the spinal column at the chest, indicating not enough control over the rib-cage for long-winded speeches. Hand signs and gestures, facial and eye expressions, other intuitive and even telepathic forms of communication, as well as "walking through" a skilled task with a teacher, were likely used more by a people less overrun with symbol-formation than humans today.

5. David Sloan Wilson, Darwin's Cathedral, pg. 1, 21 (U. of Chicago Press, 2002) Cited by Michael Shermer in The Science of Good & Evil, 2004, pg. 54, 55 "anthropological studies of meat sharing practices by all modern hunter-gatherer communities around the world. It turns out that these small bands and tribes . . . are remarkably egalitarian" see also pg. 50 – 53.
    As for chimpanzee hunters, who are also male, "Pieces of meat are doled out strategically, mostly to allies, relatives, and sexually receptive females." (Natural History, Jan. 1995, pg. 53). Upright apes were most likely even less egalitarian than this.

6. See Time, 10-8-12 "…every such group ever studied has been found to idealize altruism and punish selfishness, in everything from their mythologies to their mating practices." (Eric Michael Johnson, evolutionary anthropologist)
    Even today, in our damages condition, we can see the remaining power of the human Deep Structure. "Studies of 18-month-old toddlers show that they will almost always try to help an adult who is visibly struggling with a task, without being asked to do so…" "Worldwide, the aftermath of natural disasters are typically characterized by heroism and sharing of resources…" (both from Time, 10-8-12). See also Scientific American, 11-20-12, on 5 studies with a total of 834 participants. "The results were striking: in every single study, faster – that is more intuitive – decisions were associated with high levels of cooperation, whereas slower – that is, more reflective – decisions were associated with higher levels of selfishness."

Criteria for calling a Homo species human

1. Fully human build (e.g. "Narakatome Boy" – 1.7 million years old).

2. Fully human hands - not Australopithecine or "apith" hands – at least 1.4 million years ago (LiveScience, 12-16-13, from Carol Ward, U. of Missouri).

3. Sexual size difference not significantly different from Homo sapiens (already in place 1.7 million years ago)

4. Large enough opening in the spinal column below the neck for long, complex vocalizations (control over rib cage) – e.g. Gran Dolina, 800,000 years old.

5. Hunter-gatherer way of life – communist bands, not patriarchal gorilla/apith harems – see 3.

6. Stone tools at least early Acheulian – 1.5 to 1.8 million years ago.

7. Brain size at least 900 c.c., maybe 1000 c.c. – 1.5 to 1.8 million years ago.

8. Care for old and wounded by band – see bone diseased Homo erectus, KNM-ER 1808 – 1.7 million years old.

9. Use of fire, and control over it – around 1.5 million years ago.

10. Ability to throw far and accurately, at least in males, who hunted - about 1.8 million years ago (Nature, 6-26-13, from Neil Roach, Washington U. & Harvard U.). Combined with 2., 6., and 9., the use of fire-hardened wooden spears. Stone-tipped spears show up at least 500,000 years ago (Scientific American, 11-15-12).

The entire suite of these human abilities came together as a package, with the formation of Homo erectus, 1.8 million years ago (see punctuated equilibria). Homo habilis (probably a grab-bag term for several species), starting 2.5 million years ago, was transitional to this from Australopithecus. Homo erectus spread quickly all over the Old World almost immediately after its formation, unlike habilis or any of the "apiths". The only exception to this human package is 4., and this happened with the formation of Homo heidelbergensis, 800,000 years ago. Homo heidelbergensis also had a larger brain – in the 1100 cc to 1400 cc range, not very different from Homo sapiens.

A new Party Line has emerged in the capitalist press. Paleoanthropologists used to call Neanderthals "Homo sapiens neandertalis", i.e. an extinct race of our own species. There is some genetic evidence, in mitochondrial DNA, that they were in fact a separate but closely related species, having a common ancestor with sapiens 500,000 years ago.

Now, the capitalist press only refers to members of our genus as human if they were "behaviorally modern" – i.e. dependent on language as we know it now. This does **not** include the vast body of holistic utterances, many of them highly complex, and usually embedded in music, that was likely the language **not** as we know it of Homo neandertalis, and of our **own** species for the first 120,000 years of its existence (see Steve Mithen, The Singing Neanderthals). Nor does this include nonverbal communication – much of it highly complex and subtle, nor walking through a skilled task with a teacher, nor telepathy – all of which existed before language as we know it.

Never mind "mystical experience" (Direct Knowledge) – that is an entire subject unto itself, and requires the massive neural capacity humans have had for a **long** time.

Homo neandertalis, along with Homo erectus, have even been called "creatures" in the capitalist press, a label insulting to all but the most unevolved forms of animal life. The irony here is that our own species would have to be called a "creature" by this criteria, until 40,000 years ago when full dependence on language as we know it consolidated. The not-fully-conscious implied reasoning here is that it isn't "human" unless its civilized – patriarchy (like gorillas) and later forms of class society, hierarchy, coercion, agriculture – with a lot more work and a poorer diet, environmental destruction, disease, and famines. All the plagues of the

Fall. Classless, stateless hunter-gatherers, even **with** language as we know it, soon may be called "creatures" too.

For its part, science is finally referring to all humans (civilized or not) as a kind of animal. Our neural architecture and neurochemistry is the same as other mammals. Put more simply – other mammals have the same feelings that we do. Our neocortex is just more elaborated than any other mammal, except the sadly named "bottlenose dolphin".

Postscript:

Since the mitochondrial DNA/Out of Africa thesis (on Homo sapien origin) emerged in the mid-1980's, the hugely dominant position among paleoanthropologists went something like this: "WE Sapiens NEVER intermarried with those OTHER species. Our Sapien blood is as pure as the driven snow." Eerily echoing the oh-so-distasteful "miscegenation" fight in the U.S. South.

This brouhaha has now been settled. The genome of Neandertals and Denisovians has been sequenced and compared to living Sapiens.

"An analysis of this ancient DNA, published Wednesday in Nature, reveals that the genomes of people in New Guinea contain 4.8% Denisovian DNA." "…the scientists also found that 2.5% of the Neandertal genome is more similar to the DNA of living Europeans and Asians than to African DNA." (N.Y. Times, 12-23-10)

If two animals (and humans are a kind of animal) mate in nature and produce viable, reproductive offspring, they are **not** separate species, but subspecies of the same species. Any species with the vast spread of humans, covering most of the Old World for as much as 1.8 million years, is going to differentiate into subspecies. Like cougars, only 1 million years old, in the New World. But there is still genetic mixing. It should also be noted here that the Neandertal genome is 99.84% identical to living Sapiens.

The mysterious Denisovian people may be none other than Homo heidelbergensis. Scientists recently sequenced the mitochondrial DNA of 400,000 year old human fossils from Spain (Sima de los Huescos) and found it more similar to Denisovian DNA than to Neanderthal (A.P./S.F. Chronicle, 12-5-13). The sequenced Denisovian DNA came from Siberia, and is around 40,000 years old. Neanderthals sub-speciated around 250,000 years ago in eastern Europe and central Asia. The oldest clearly Sapien fossil, the Idaltu cranium, 160,000 years old, comes from Ethiopia.

There is even a Homo erectus cranium, from Java, that is as young as 27,000 years old. Young enough to be DNA sequenced, but the DNA may have degraded in the wet tropical climate. Homo erectus, as a species, is 1.8 million years old.

I predict that the correct taxonomy for living humans will be this: Homo erectus sapiens.

The Fall:
Patriarchy – The First Class Society

A paper you **must** read is LINEAGE SOCIETIES – THE ORIGIN OF WOMEN'S OPPRESSION, by Nicole Chevillard and Sebastien Leconte. It is in Women's Work, Men's Property, edited by Stephanie Coontz and Peta Henderson (Verso Press, 1986). It is very well researched.

There are plenty of "living fossils" of the first class societies, a lot more than the relatively few "living fossils" of normal (hunter-gatherer-permaculturist) human societies. They are **not** civilized. **No** cities, states, or written language. Many are still one-third dependent on hunting and gathering. But they are without question class societies, the consolidation of the Fall. I call them Early Patriarchy. They laid the foundation for what became civilization.

The progression of the Fall, very briefly, looks something like this: First, the decay of our original direct relationship with Reality, enabled by the consolidation of language as we know it, 40,000 years ago.

(This unprecedented development was a result of extreme selective pressure never before faced by humans. Between 100,000 and 10,000 years ago, the Earth's climate became violently unstable – jerking suddenly from ice ages to brief interglacial warmings like our longer present Holocene. Local extinctions of humans became common. Adaption to sudden, extreme changes in habitat – including having to move suddenly and far, would have required a more advanced level of abstraction than enabled by the Original Language, even the very advanced forms of it that existed by then. It is likely to have also encouraged an incipient distrust of the rest of nature (1).)

Then the consolidation of Early Patriarchy, or Neolithic society, 10,000 years ago, in certain places. Then city-states/early civilization, then the successive forms of class society/economic slavery since. Finally, the vast mess we have now – with a viral growth curve of a degenerate population and a relentless degradation of the biosphere this population depends on for survival.

All these plagues didn't **suddenly** happen when a woman named Eve bit into an apple. Notice that a mythical women gets blamed for the Fall, when it was Early Patriarchy that consolidated it. The victors, as the saying goes, write history. Appropriately named His Story. And (Surprise! Surprise!) it was not long after enslaving women that men began enslaving each other.

A qualifier on the consolidation of language as we know it, 40,000 years ago. It was more similar to the Original Language than modern English. A young Pomo (a northern California tribe of the Original People here), learning the language of his tribe, says it is deeper than modern English.

A powerful remnant of the Original Language is music. This is why the best psychedelic music of 1965-1971, and the best spiritual music/mantra, is so powerful and enduring. You **must** read The Singing Neanderthals, by Stephen Mithen (Harvard University Press, 2006). He posits that the musical ability of Neanderthals (and Sapiens before 40,000 years ago) was vastly more developed than humans alive today – part of what their huge cranial capacity was being used for before language as we know it.

A qualifier on the gender relations of normal (hunter-gatherer-permaculturist) human societies. In tribes where men brought in most or all of the food, men dominated. This was an outlier, restricted to boreal or tundra climates. Intuit ("Eskimo") women are not treated very well. By contrast, among the Original People of California, where women brought in 60%-70% of the food, plus all medicinal plants, most shamen/healers were women, and it was common for women to be chiefs. And Hadza women, in what is now Tanzania, do not take any shit from their men.

(1.) Late in the Upper Paleolithic, in Europe, a disturbing development emerged – the mass killing of prey species with cliff drives. There had been occasional, limited practice of this by Neanderthals and earlier Sapiens, but in Europe this now became common and voracious. (Kirkpatric Sale, After Eden, pg. 79) Humans had **never** behaved like this before, and neither does any other apex predator – they only kill what they need to live (in humans, this included frozen or jerked meat for storage). And humans had **long** been the final apex predator – we could take down a rhinoceros at least 500,000 years ago, which not even a pride of lions can do. I also know for a fact that the Upper Paleolithic Original People ("wild Indians") of Northern and Central California never conducted mass killings either. They were highly aware of carrying capacity and attuned to the rest of nature. These mass killings, a warning of much uglier things to come, stupidly extincted the very prey species that humans depended on.

Family life before and after the Fall: Stages of Social Dis-Integration!

SOCIAL ORDER: Early (Paleolithic) communism – pre-Fall
FAMILY STRUCTURE: Tribal band
SOME KEY CHARACTERISTICS: Based on both blood ties and tight friendship (buddies for life), permanent and rooted in tribe. Matrilinial, often with brother of mother helping to raise kids. Plenty of allo-parenting. Sexuality often non-monogamous (and bisexual), rooted in permanent friendship and integrated into life.

SOCIAL ORDERS: Fall and post-Fall. Early (Neolithic) class society – i.e. patriarchy, slavery, feudalism, earliest capitalism.
FAMILY STRUCTURE: Patriarchal extended family
SOME KEY CHARACTERISTICS: Based on blood ties alone, permanent and rooted in community. Women subjugated and even viewed as property of men. Monogamous sexuality – usually forced with double standard exempting men.

SOCIAL ORDER: Middle capitalism.
FAMILY STRUCTURE: Patriarchal nuclear family
SOME KEY CHARACTERISTICS: Based on blood ties alone, permanent but often not rooted in community - frequent moving. Combined with smaller family, this means greater isolation (and more potential for conflict and abuse), plus more complete subordination to the "needs" of exploiting class.

SOCIAL ORDER: Late capitalism (sliding into End Times!)
"FAMILY" STRUCTURE: hookups, serial infatuation, sexual "scenes"
SOME KEY CHARACTERISTICS: Both transience and isolation, with ascendancy of narcissistic disorders (and increasingly unreal search for "The One"). Split-off, fragmented, hyper-cathected pseudo-sexuality – as

compulsive acting-out of primarily pre-gender/sexual conflicts. Almost total absorption of the most intimate aspects of life by Late Capitalism, and disconnection from any decent capacity to raise up human young.

Regeneration

First Stage
SOCIAL ORDER: Self-management/working class rule
FAMILY STRUCTURE: Egalitarian extended family
SOME KEY CHARACTERISTICS: Beginning organic regeneration of non-patriarchal tribal band-like family, based in work-life (long-term membership in worker-owned/self-managed enterprise), and neighborhood (permanently affordable and often cooperative home ownership).

Advanced Stage
SOCIAL ORDER: Classless society/The Return
FAMILY STRUCTURE: Tribal band
SOME KEY CHARACTERISTICS: Full regeneration of normal human life/intimacy with the rest of nature. Appropriation of some radically altered technology as seen fit by normal humans with completely regenerated/intact Deep Structures. What is now called "mystical experience" will be universal and frequent. Quality of life so deep as to be unimaginable to most humans alive today.

What is at stake now

Something else is likely to be going on with class society besides damage to normal human Deep Structure gene expression. This would be the **re-activation** of shut-down genes from the upright-ape line that the human line evolved out of (a throw-back, or atavism, to the Australopithecenes, or apiths for short). As discussed before, two fundamental traits (among several others) distinguish the human line from the upright-ape line: strong egalitarianism and radically higher intelligence in humans.

Part of what had happened by the time that the human line consolidated with the formation of Homo erectus, around 1.8 million years ago, was the **suppression** of a lot of the earlier upright-ape DNA by the more recently evolved human DNA. Among other things, this is why our males are no longer half-again the size of our females. A lot of what evolutionarily newer DNA does is "switch off" older, obsolete DNA. This is why whales and dolphins no longer have the legs of the land mammals they evolved out of, in 3 stages, long ago.

Class society may **re-activate** older DNA associated with the severely hierarchical upright apes that lived for at least 2 million years before the human line even **began** emerging 2.5 million years ago. The two lines co-existed for a long time. The last of the upright apes, the robusts (Paranthropus), died out by 800,000 years ago, about the time Homo heidelbergensis emerged. Homo heidelbergensis had a cranial capacity in the 1100 cc – 1400 cc range, very close to Homo sapiens. Paranthropus had a cranial capacity of about 500 cc.

When humans degenerated into class society, our cranial capacity shrank by 20%, and our bodies regressed towards (though far from all the way to) upright-ape proportions – longer torso and shorter legs. Regression in human brain **organization** as well as size is almost certain. It takes less intelligence to be a cog in a slave society than it takes to be a multi-skilled, highly present, hunter-gatherer-permaculturist, with high self-management capacity, in an intimate, egalitarian society. Most of all, it takes more intelligence to be capable of receiving what has been called mystical experience, or Direct Knowledge.

Damaged human Deep Structure gene expression, a **lot** of it involving, to various degrees, critical-effect periods, combined with the likely re-activation of suppressed upright-ape DNA, helps to explain the stubborn entrenchment of class society. This entrenchment is very **recent** – just the last 5000 – 10,000 years, after nearly 2 million years of freedom. Add to this learned helplessness, internalization of class-enemy values/ideology, and force of habit. And we can now add to long-standing damage to human gene expression more recent damage caused by pollution – endocrine-disruptors and neurotoxins key among them, and progressive brain atrophy/damage caused by techie addiction. The results of all this mess are then claimed to be "human nature" by the PR shills/propagandists of capitalism (1) (2).

We are allowing ourselves to be degraded into a starkly inhuman condition. And this process is progressive – it gets relentlessly worse, like alcoholism/drug addiction, if we allow it to go on. This is what is at stake now. Class war, particularly at its more advanced level – a war between class society and the **complete emancipation of humans**, is in essence a war between the inhuman and the human (3).

What would the inhuman look like in the not very distant future? Degrading humans will be artificially bifurcated into two separate species. There will be genetic enhancements, other bioengineering enhancements, artificial intelligence implants and connections, and various nanotechnology applications only affordable to at most the wealthiest 5%. Survellance, manipulation, and control technologies we are only beginning to see now will be used on the rest of us, as the continuing degradation of human nature deepens (techie addiction being a recent emerging example). Add all this to the horrifying wealth/income disparity depicted in the movie Elysium.

A quote from Winston's torture-master in George Orwell's 1984 is instructive: "Do you want to know what the future will look like? Imagine the heel of a boot grinding a man's face – **forever"**. If we do not destroy class society, it will morph into something unimaginably more horrifying than anything we have ever seen.

1. Consider the so-called "herd instinct" in humans. There is no such thing. Not even apes have this. The herd instinct is only found in the least intelligent mammals, and it is a stark testament to our degraded condition that it is attributed to humans. The grinding daily commute found in many U.S. megopoli is basically a twice-a-day, slow-motion mass cattle-run. We are allowing ourselves to be reduced to **livestock** for the wealthy, here to feed their monstrous addiction. Many other examples can be found in degenerate mass society.

2. As for neurotoxins, check **this** out: Several studies have demonstrated that the phaseout of lead in gasoline, which began in the late 1970's, "may have been responsible for up to **half** of the extraordinary and otherwise unexplained drop in crime that occurred in the 1990's. Tens of millions of children, particularly poor children in big cities, had grown up with high levels of lead, which interfered with their neural development from the 1950's to the late 1970's." (Jonathan Haidt, The Righteous Mind, pg. 349, citing Carpenter and Nevin, 2010, Nevin, 2000, Reyes, 2007.)

3. Not to disparage all non-human beings. Cougar-kitty (my totem animal) is a magnificently free and independent being, bowing before no master. As for humans, one of the biggest questions the Yahi (Ishi's People) had about the European invaders who were genociding them was this: Are they human? Are they the same species as us, or even a normal form of life? Even with their strange pale skin, strange body hair, and bad smell, they **looked** a lot like humans. And they had **more** advanced technology, clearly indicating human-level intelligence. But they did not behave like humans. The Yahi's neighbors, like the Wintu or the Maidu, were not the same People as the Yahi. But they were without question human. They behaved like humans.

HUMAN EVOLUTION BIBLIOGRAPHY

DAWN OF MAN
C 2000 Robin McKie Dorling Kindersley Publishing, Inc.

FROM LUCY TO LANGUAGE
Text c 1996 Donald C. Johanson & Blake Edgar Simon & Schuster

THE LAST NEANDERTAL
C 1995 Ian Tattersal Macmillan/ Simon & Schuster

THE WISDOM OF THE BONES
C 1996 Alan Walker and Pat Shipman Vintage Books/ Random House

NO WAY OUT ? in RUNNING ON EMPTINESS
C 2002 John Zerzan Feral House

ELEMENTS OF REFUSAL
C 1999 John Zerzan C.A.L. Press

THE SYMBOLIC SPECIES
C 1997 Terrence Deakon W.W. Norton & Co., Inc.

JAVA MAN
C 2000 Garniss H. Curtis, Carl C. Swisher, Roger Lewin U. of Chicago Press

FAIRWEATHER EDEN
C 1997 Michael Pitts and Mark Roberts Fromm Intl. Publishing Corp.

THE ORIGIN OF HUMANKIND
Richard Leakey c 1994 Basic Books/ Harper Collins Publishers, Inc.

ORIGINS RECONSIDERED
Richard Leakey and Roger Lewin c 1992 Sherma B.V. Bantam Doubleday
Dell Publishing Group, Inc.

BECOMING HUMAN
C 1998 Ian Tattersal Harvest/ Harcourt Brace & Co.

WHAT IT MEANS TO BE 98% CHIMPANZEE
Jonathan Marks c 2002 Regents of the U. of Calif. U. of CA Press

MAPPING HUMAN HISTORY
C 2002 Steve Olson Houghton Mifflin Co.

STRANGER IN A NEW LAND in Scientific American, Nov. 2003 Kate
Wong

HUMAN EVOLUTION READER compiled by Roger C. Newman
For Anthropology 1, Vista College, Berkeley, CA

QUARRY
C 1993 Noel T. Boaz The Free Press/ Macmillan

TIMEWALKERS
C 1993 Clive Gamble Harvard U. Press

THE OHLONE WAY
C 1978 Malcolm Margolin Heyday Books

ISHI, LAST OF HIS TRIBE
C 1964 Theodora Kroeber Parnassus Press

ISHI IN TWO WORLDS

C 1961 Regents of the U. of CA
Authored by Theodora Kroeber

THE NATURAL WORLD of the CALIFORNIA INDIANS
C 1980 Regents of the U. of CA U. of CA Press
Authored by Robert f. Heizer & Albert B. Elsasser

WOMEN'S WORK, MEN'S PROPERTY
C 1986 Stephanie Coontz and Peta Henderson Verso Press
(origins of patriarchy/class society)

GOD IS RED
C 1973 Vine Deloria, Jr. Dell Publishing Co.

TENDING THE WILD
C 2005 M. Kat Anderson U. of Calif. Press

THE HADZA
C 2010 The Regents of U. of Calif. By Frank Marlowe

ANIMISM Respect for the Living World
C 2006 Graham Harvey Columbia U. Press

THE SINGING NEANDERTHALS
C 2006 Stephen Mithen Harvard U. Press

99%'ers. The economics of our present (and future) situation

Much has been said about how the occupy movement lacked focus, specific demands, or identitified leaders. This involves a **lot** of embedded assumptions.

I will try to clarify some basics.

The focus, for all these young people, most of whom have no decent future within the metastasized cancer that is Late Capitalism, is a gut revulsion against the entire system itself. This has wide sympathy, tho not a clear majority.

These young have not had the time to learn how to destroy the grip of this monstrosity on their lives. I'm 54, and have had the time to learn this body of skills. This is **not** a demand. It is a fact on the ground. There was **no** social solution for me in the '80's and '90's. I had to fight them on my own. **I won**.

Conditions were bad when I was their age, they are worse now, and they will git much worse. **That** is a certainty.

The problem is not "capitalism run amok" (to quote my liberal union-member Mom). It is the **inherent nature** of capitalism to run amok.

To cite a huge specific example, the real debt load of U.S. finance capital is now a closely guarded secret. I can't git any current facts on it. It was already substantially larger than the 2011 Federal Govt. debt, back in 2008. In 2008, the aggregate debt load of the whole U.S. economy was 4.3 times annual U.S. GDP (3.7 times by another measure), vs. 1.25 to 1.5 times from 1951 to 1981 (Haver, Federal Reserve, quoted in The Market Oracle, 2-2-13) (A clue: the loan guarantees the Fed. has made to U.S. finance capital are in the vicinity of $16 to $18 **trillion**. Mark my words: these vast guarantees will be paid for with **printed** money. This is the last scam they have left.)

From Sept. 2008 through all of 2009, the entire U.S. capitalist system was only saved from complete implosion by the most massive State intervention since World War 2, and an exponentially larger State intervention than **any** in peacetime in U.S. history. Adding the Wall St. bailout, the Obama stimulus, and $2.3 trillion of newly printed money (QE) together, the equivalent of 28% of the **entire** annual U.S. GDP was injected into the economy in about a year. The economy would have contracted by at least this much more than it did in this period, had this not been done. We would have a new word in our vocabulary: hyperdepression. Even with all this money thrown at it, the crippled U.S. economy remains chronically dependent on an injection of $1 trillion in newly printed money each year, or about 7% of annual GDP. (1)

To make a long story short – the Late Capitalist economy is being crushed by **way** too much debt, and **way** too much speculative capital sloshing around in the top 1%. These vast structural problems are not going away anytime soon. (2)

When the inevitable results of this come to pass, we will need a massively practiced body of **acts**, far more than we will need to make demands.

Aside from immediate practical needs, the very idea of "demands" assumes a dependence on the class enemy that has **no** need to exist.

A worker-owned, self-managed enterprise is **not** a demand. It is a self-created **fact** on the ground. The neighborhood assemblies in Argentina, in 2001, who made sure everyone had enough to eat in a Depression as bad as ours in 1932, were **not** a demand. They were a **fact** on the ground.

We need to take/create what we need, not "militantly" whine for it.

We can link specific, concrete demands to self-created facts on the ground, but we cannot depend on these demands.

When we own and manage the enterprises that we work for, own our homes, free from bone-crushing debt (enabled by limited-equity housing co-ops and community development credit unions), cannot be viciously gouged for healthcare, and have no student loans or credit card debt – there is no need for us to whine to the government to try to tax the rich. **Because the rich will not be able to take any of the wealth we create in the first place**.

(1) What is interesting here is that the Tea Party movement, supported by about 20% of the electorate as of 2013, **opposed** all these measures, the very measures that (temporarily) saved a deeply rotten capitalist system from itself. The "pragmatic" wing of the GOP, with ruling-class backing, knows better. But **never** let hard realities **spoil** a dearly held ideology! 40 years of incessant, very well financed "free market" propaganda have come back to bite the capitalist oligarchy in the ass.

The Tea Party is dead on about one thing: the vast rescue measures did not **solve** anything, and in fact made the deep structural pathology of Late Capitalism even worse.

(2) Some recent updates on the structural pathology of U.S. capitalism: "As (Peter) Atwater points out (banks, hedge funds, and money managers) are now using record levels of debt and leverage to buy up stocks, since the Fed's money dump (printing $85 billion a month) keeps interest rates so low." (Time, 10-14-13) See The Economist, 10-4-13, on hidden levels of corporate debt, and chronically low levels of productive investment. Money-printing (QE) will account for 75% of new govt. borrowing in 2013 at present levels. Over half of the federal debt in public hands is held by foreigners, and just under a third of this debt has a maturity of less than a year (Niall Ferguson, in The Wall St. Journal, 10-4-13). "The wealthiest 1% of U.S. households are saving 30% of their take-home pay, **triple** what they were saving in 2008." (AP, 10-6-13, citing July 2013 data from American Express Publishing/ Harrison Group) (Why even the capitalist oligarchy **itself** has such deep, abiding faith in its own rotten system!)

A Depression Starting in 2016?

Say it RIGHT! Don't say "contained depression (for now)", say "a recovery held back by secular stagnation". Don't say "money-printing", say "quantitative easing".

While trying to snow the rest of us with happy-talk, the wealthy and their corporations are acting as if they expect a full-blown Depression. The savings rate of the richest 1% has seen a sustained increase from 10% in 2008 to 30% (preceding footnote 2). Most of this is going into "hot money" seeking the highest short-term return, not long-term productive investment. For example, the average holding period for a stock is now all of 7 months, vs. 7 years 40 years ago (1).

In addition to chronically low corporate productive investment (preceding footnote 2), corporations are hoarding cash - $1.64 trillion as of early 2014 (2). This is enabled by grinding down workers to raise profit – 10.5% of GDP in 2013 vs. 6.4% in 1996. Profit is only one source of return for the wealthy, and wages as a share of GDP have fallen from 51.3% in 1970 to 42.5% in 2013. (3) More than $2 trillion in corporate merger/acquisition deals have been announced for 2014 as of Aug., a 70% increase over an already high 2013. (13)

"Households are repairing their balance-sheets." More happy-talk. U.S. household debt fell from $12.3 trillion in 2008 to $11.2 trillion in 2013 (a vast decline of 9%) and is now rapidly rising again (4). Nearly all of this small decline was a result of foreclosures and short-sales on housing. In the same period federal govt. debt doubled from $9 trillion in 2007 to $17.6 trillion as of July 2014 (5). A bloated, taxpayer-subsidized financial sector, with all its exotic, opaque hot-money derivatives (and other shell-games) hiding vast debt, sucks 30% of all corporate profit while creating just 6% of U.S. jobs (6). "The gross size of all bank derivatives positions now exceeds $650 TRILLION, more than 9 times global GDP." (James Rickards, 2014 (7)) Derivatives are a lot of what brought on the first stage of the crisis in 2008-9.

The deep structural pathology of U.S. capitalism is actually worse than in 1929. Then, there was little federal govt. debt, and the federal govt. was running surpluses. There hadn't already been vast bailouts and money-printing. The U.S. economy was running consistent, healthy trade surpluses. The financial sector had a hard capital cushion of 25% vs. 6%-8% now. The aggregate debt load of the economy was bad, but is worse now. Maldistribution of wealth and income was as bad as now (and now is getting worse). At the same time, an accumulation of deep structural pathology in all the major, highly interconnected capitalist economies – U.S., Europe including the U.K., China, and Japan, is converging (10). It is the Perfect Storm.

All the "little people" in the U.S. are very ill-prepared to cope with a full-blown Depression. A 2014 Fed survey shows that just 1 in 3 American workers under age 60 have enough savings to cover even 3 months of expenses, when even now, after 5 years of "recovery", the mean duration of unemployment is 8 months. (8) If most people thought about how vulnerable they are, they would be paralyzed by fear. This will greatly change if people respond to events collectively. Many among the age 25-34 set are coping with an already bad situation by living with their parents – 24%, up from 11% in 1980 (9).

As of this writing (8-29-14), the highly debt-loaded Chinese real-estate bubble, the largest in human history, began to collapse about 8 months ago. The impact is already spreading to the rest of China's economy. The Euro zone has been nearing outright deflation, with inflation around 0.5% (annualized) for most of 2014, and a feeble "recovery" has halted. Deflation and economic contraction will raise the cost of Europe's already huge aggregate debt load. Housing prices in the greater London area fell 6% in the single month of Aug., the 3rd consecutive monthly decline (11). The severely bloated U.K. financial sector, the debt of which raises the aggregate debt load of the U.K. economy to 12 times annual GDP (10), is highly interconnected to the world economy. Contagion awaits! Companies in the

U.S. Fortune 500 generate nearly half of their sales abroad; for the entire U.S. economy, its 14%, up from 9% in 2002 (12).

FOOTNOTES

1) Time, 7-21-14

2) HuffPost, 8-15-14

3) Yahoo Finance, 8-19-14

4) Economist, 8-2-14

5) Terry Burnham, cited in HuffPost, 7-16-14

6) Time, 7-21-14

7) The Death of Money, James Rickards, 2014, pg.11

8) HuffPost, 8-7-14, Motley Fool, 8-10-14

9) Pew Research, cited in LA Times, 7-18-14

10) See next chapter for aggregate debt loads of various economies.

11) Reuters, 8-18-14

12) Associated Press, 8-29-14, Associated Press, 8-15-14

13) USA Today, 8-26-14 While the accelerating frenzy of these deals, partly fuelled by low interest rates, generate big $$$ for top management and investors, they may in part be preparation for a Depression. Depressions force consolidation through bankruptcies and distressed mergers. Avoid the rush! Consolidate now!

To Occupy Wall Street (7-23-12)

Good point (re: the estimated $18 **trillion** of assets the U.S. rich have stashed in offshore havens). But "abusive forms of capitalism"? Spare us the liberal whining.

Occupy fetishized a tactic, the police adapted, and its over.

We need to be more fluid, and unpredictable. Think tactical flexibility.

Class war is asymmetrical, like the full-blown shooting war now going on in Syria.

We can disable Wall St. and K St. without **any** 24-7 occupation, far less any violence.

We shut down the S.F. financial district (if only for a day) in March of 2003. 30,000 of us, without any 24-7 occupation. We were fluid, innovative, and numerous. The police were helpless.

It was only for a day, because there was no draft for the invasion of Iraq. None of us really had any "skin in the game". How different with our economic situation here at home, which is likely to git much worse.

As for offshore "assets", the class enemy can move paper "assets" to the Cayman Islands, but they **can't** move the hard assets that back them – fixed capital, land, and housing. In time, these paper "assets" are likely to lose most of their value anyway. Read Currency Wars, by James Rickards. Also study, if you haven't already, the neighborhood assemblies of Argentina in 2001, during their Great Depression.

Brief overview of economic data

Much has already been reported on the relentless grinding-down of America's "middle class" (code for working class) over the last 35 years, and the simultaneous runaway engorgement of the already ludicrously wealthy. No one seems to have a **clue** what to **do** about it. This book is an effort to rectify that. If this is not done, see the movie Elysium for a sneak preview of your children's exciting future (and yours, should you be young enough to live another 40 or 50 years).

A brief overview as a reminder:

Aggregate debt load of some major economies, as a % of annual GDP, 2011:
(excluding financial sector)
Japan – 475%, U.K. – 360%, 1200% including financial sector, France – 330%,
U.S.A. – 310%, Germany – 255%, China – 185%
(Wall St. Journal, 5-24-13, Economist, 9-14-13)

MEDIAN household net worth, 2010 or latest available:
Italy - $212,000 France - $144,000 Germany - $63,000 (all at 6-15-12 exchange rates)
U.S.A. - $61,000 (2013) (Economist, 6-15-13)
Within the U.S.A.: whites - $113,149 Latinos - $6325 blacks - $5677 (Pew Research, 2009)

Average U.S. net worth, adding in the rich and near-rich, was $522,000 as of June 2013, 8.6 times higher than the median. Put another way, this is what each U.S. household would have if all the private net worth was divided equally. (Economist, 6-22-13)

The U.S. had 3.4 million households with at least $1 million in investable assets (excluding home), in 2012, out of a total U.S. population of around 330 million, including children. (Economist, 6-22-13) 70% of these deprived darlings do not consider themselves wealthy. (CNN Money, 7-24-13)

The 2012 share of total income going to the richest 1% was 19.3%, up from 7.7% in 1974, and the highest since 1928 (1 year before the Great

Depression started). (From another source, AP 1-27-14, the 2012 income share of the top 1% was put at 22.5%.) The income share going to the richest 10% was 48.2%, the highest ever recorded in records going back to 1913, making the U.S. almost as bad as Brazil in the 1990's. (AP and WSJ, 9-10-13, from Emmanuel Saez, U.C. Berkeley) And this is just the income we know about – never mind the 1 million offshore bank accounts the U.S. wealthy had in 2001 (S.F. Chronicle, GIT DATE), plus many other shell-games.

"If Californians lose their jobs or have some sort of other emergency arise, 46% couldn't cover their expenses for 3 months, according to a national study released Thur. by the Corporation for Enterprise Development."(S.F. Chronicle, 1-30-14) 75% of Americans aged 45-64 have **less** than $27,000 in their retirement accounts; this includes 33% of Americans aged 45-64 with **no** retirement account at all.(WSJ, 1-29-14)

It should be noted here that distribution of wealth, plus low debt, is more critical than distribution of income. Modest wealth plus low debt, plus freedom from bosses, enables quality of life.

Take myself: The monthly interest payment on my tiny mortgage is all of $50 (I don't know **how** I manage!), and I have a beautiful view over a big park and the big hills above Vallejo right out my top-floor landscaped deck. The trees in the park stop the freeway noise, over a mile away. I've got no truck payments, credit-card debt, or student loans. My pay for doing healthy outdoor physical work, much of it requiring creativity, is twice the hourly rate I would get doing the same work for a boss. All this enables me the time and freedom to cultivate a "charmed renaissance lifestyle", including the time to research and write this book.

Now that great Avatar- economist of the Right, Hayeck (who actually had some useful things to say about running the productive base) insists that we **must** have the inherited wealthy, because only they have the time and resources to cultivate fine aesthetic and philosophical sensitivities. You can flush that one down the toilet of history. Git **rid** of capitalism, and we'll all have time for that and far better things.

What's wrong with the 99% slogan

The top 1% (by income) got a **minimum** of $390,000 a year in 2012 (Keplinger, 1-22-14). The next 4% below that are **hardly** middle-class – an income of $168,000 to $389,000 in 2012, and in most cases, investable assets (excluding home) of at **least** $1 million – the wealthiest 5% of households have at **least** this. This next-richest 4% group is not the core capitalist oligarchy – it does not decide what goes on – but its aggregate wealth is nearly as large. This class heavily includes those who execute capitalist policy: upper management, including Personnel Control ("human resource") specialists, corporate lawyers and PR specialists, lobbyists, investment bankers, smaller real-estate speculators/landlords, lawyers, accountants, and PR men for individuals in the top 1%, union-busting specialists, and political operatives for the oligarchy. They are **not** the family doctors, dentists, or college professors of the traditional upper-middle class. They are greedier, wealthier, and **far** more often occupied with parasitic/malignant activity. I refer to them as the Inner Yuppie Minions (of the core capitalist oligarchy), and they are mostly a class enemy, **not** a middle layer.

The next 5% below this (by income), $121,000 to $168,000 in 2012, are a more mixed lot. Altogether, the wealthiest 10% of U.S. households had 74% of U.S. wealth in 2012 (Saez and Zucman, 2014). The bottom 80% had all of 7% (Henry Blodget, Business Insider, 11-29-13). This is what economic slavery looks like.

Along the same lines, debt-peonage is **not** home-ownership. A dishonest statistic is that about 64% of U.S. households (2013) are home "owners". At the top of the reflation of the housing bubble, in April 2014, 20% of home "owners" with a mortgage, or about 15% of all home "owners", still owed **more** than their home was worth. The real number of effectively underwater home "owners" is much larger. To be able to move and buy another house, you need to pay the realtor commission, your share of closing costs, and then have at least 10% of the sale price left over (assuming you have stellar credit) for the down-payment on a new home. Debt-peonage has long been one of the main tools the wealthy oligarchy uses to enslave us and strip us of the wealth we create.

Some notes on housing costs

There are a number of references to "bone-crushing mortgages" and "rent gouging" in this book. In most of California, where I have lived all my life, this is a big to severe problem, and has been since the late 1970's. It is less so in many other parts of the U.S.

A few statistics: On rent, in 2011, 28% of renter households in all the U.S. spend **over half** their gross household income on rent. An additional 23% spend 31% to 50% of gross income on rent. (Joint Center for Housing Studies, Harvard U., cited by Kathleen Pender in the S.F. Chronicle, 12-10-13) California data isn't a lot worse, but with 2 qualifiers – more households here, about 48%, are renters, and many households here double-up or otherwise crowd to make housing costs manageable. "Opportunity awaits! Did you know that even your living room can be rented out?"

Trullia Trends did a study on home ownership affordability (10-10-13), based on house prices and median household incomes in each urban area (many of them megopoli broken into smaller county-based parts). But this study assumes a down-payment of 20%. Even in the most affordable Midwest, this comes to $40,000 to $55,000 for the top of the "affordable" part of total housing in question. Also a 30-year mortgage, which has the worst total interest cost – see and total loan amortization/progress data to see how bad this is.

That aberrant era: 1948-1973

A new book titled Capital in the 21st Century, by Thomas Piketty, has been getting a fair amount of press recently. Its central point is that the broadly-based prosperity of the 1948-1973 period (real wages in the U.S. more than doubled) was an anomaly in the history of capitalist domination.

What we have now is the way capitalism normally and inherently operates, and it is going to get a lot worse. I've been harping on this for some time, but Piketty's book is a 700-page tome with an immense mass of data going back 300 years. I highly recommend it to all these U.S. progressives who have been endlessly pining for that bygone aberrant era.

That era was only tolerated by the capitalist oligarchy because it was in shock after 2 genocidal world wars, the Great Depression, and all the associated social upheaval. It was allowed **only** to buy time. It was **never** a social contract of any kind, and **anyone** who believed otherwise was a fool. Most of the wealthy **never** accepted strong unions, even modestly effective (as opposed to nominal) progressive taxation (1), or a serious social safety net. They just bided their time until the opportunity to grind down and destroy all these could be created. This started becoming possible in 1978-80. If it continues, the consummation of this will be the voucherization/privatization of Medicare – which will effectively sic the chargemaster on the 65 + set (see Health"care" "cost" in the U.S.A., in this book), and finally, the privatization of Social Security – which will hand over all that cash flow to the Wall St. scum who brought us the crisis of 2008.

(1) The 400 highest-income taxpayers in 2007, each with an average income of $300 **million** for the year, paid only 17% of their total incomes in taxes that year. (Robert Reich, Aftershock, pg. 131-132) It should also be noted here that MediCare is financed by a flat tax on wages/salaries (effectively regressive), and Social Security, with its cap on the wage/salary income that gets flat-taxed for it, by an **absolutely** regressive tax. Neither are funded by **any** tax on capital gains, which go mostly to the rich.

2 major work surveys

Now as if all that dreary information wasn't enough, there's **more!** (This chapter **is** about the **problem**, not the solution.)

"For most of us, in short, work is a depleting, dispiriting experience, and in some obvious ways, it is getting worse." "The rise of digital technology is perhaps the biggest influence, exposing us to an unprecedented flood of information and requests that we feel compelled to read and respond to at all hours of the day and night."

	Do have	Don't have
Regular time for creative or strategic thinking	18%	70%
Ability to focus on one thing at a time	21%	66%
Opportunities to do what is most enjoyed	33%	60%
Level of meaning and significance	36%	50%
A sense of community	35%	49%
Opportunities for learning and growth	38%	48%

(2013, worldwide survey, The Energy Project, reported in N.Y. Times, 6-1-14)

". . . 80% of Americans feel stressed by at least one thing on the job." They are, in order (1)"Overall, long commutes and low pay tied as the No. 1 workplace stressors" (2) "closely followed by unreasonable workloads" (3) "Annoying co-workers ranked 3rd." (4) "next came poor work-life balance . . ."

(Harris Interactive, for Everest College, reported in S.F. Chronicle, 5-23-14)

Welcome to The Disease of Late Capitalism, "the **best** of all possible worlds!" To read about a big part of the cure, refer to Chapter 19: Transitional Economics: Where Working People are Taking Power Now.

Health "care" "cost" in the U.S.A.

Re: "Health law's reality sets in" (West County Times, 10-6-13)

This article sickened me, but did not surprise me at all. And I'm one of the people who stands to get subsidized health insurance. **Please** run a summary of Time magazine's expose of U.S. healthcare charges: Bitter Pill, in their 3-4-13 issue. As they put it, the relevant question isn't "Who pays?", but **Why does it cost so much?**

See the appendix to the Eden chapter: The Diseases of Late Capitalism.

How the U.S. Healthcare Fraud and Extortion Racket Works

Healthcare charges from providers are based on a monstrosity called the chargemaster. This routinely hyperinflates charges to 8 to 20 **times** the actual costs. Then add the fee-for-service structure which incentivizes **quantity** of care rather than **quality** (more $$$). Add the longstanding neglect of preventative care/education, because far more $$$ can be had by gouging people when they get sick. What device makers sell to providers at is a closely guarded secret, so the provider markup on this is too. And the providers are usually invested in the device makers. Do not be fooled by "non-profit" status or in-house provision, these are among the worst offenders. Accounting shell-games and badly overpaid administration (much of it in perks) conceal vast blood-sucking. Insurers get a discount off the chargemaster, but that is a closely guarded secret too. Experts guess it is 30% to 40%.

As The Economist put it, the U.S. healthcare system "has all the transparency of a concrete bunker". An iron law: the lack of transparency is **directly** proportional to the level of corruption. Then add to all this mess the 30% bureaucratic overhead health insurers create.

This vast sea of vicious greed, corruption, and secrecy then shows up as your deliteful health insurance premium bill, or the one your employer gets. Plus out-of-pocket charges, co-pays, and caps on coverage.

Obamacare barely touches nearly any of this, which is why all these premium subsidies are needed. This is in great part covered by gouging people above 400% of the Federal poverty line even worse than they are already gouged now. This shifts "costs" that don't really even exist.

Again, read the Time magazine expose, 3-4-13. Check out the blue-collar guy in his '30's who got an $89,000 back-ache.

That bizarre conspiracy theory
(and its unconscious basis in present reality)

You've probably heard it. We are all ruled by a conspiracy of highly intelligent reptiles that shape-shift into human form. It involves the British royal family, the Rothschilds, and the Satanic realm (a parallel universe that intersects with our known universe). Laughable on the face of it. Conspiracy theories in general flourish when more and more wealth/power concentrate into the hands of the richest 1%, and most of the rest of us have less and less real control over our own lives. Clearly our present condition. These conspiracy theories usually have big chunks of truth in them, or are symbolically true, and are then elaborated into paranoid fantasies.

The real ruling class is not monolithic. It contains ideological and sectoral factions, and individual exceptions to what is generally true.

As for the reptilian business, check this out. Individuals with hard-core narcissistic personalities, and the very closely related sociopathic (also called psychopathic) personalities, have no real capacity for empathy, love, or remorse, and from this no real conscience. They can fake these, with their usually good to excellent surface charm and social functioning, in order to manipulate and exploit people, but that is all. They pass lie detector tests with ease. Their desire-drives are malignant and insatiable.

Neurobiologically, these individuals have practically no oxytocin system, the biggest biological basis for the capacity to empathize or love in mammals. In normal mammals, highly social species, like prairie voles (a.k.a. prairie dogs), who live in tight communities and form life-long monogamous relationships, the brain is densely packed with oxytocin receptors. Unsocial mammals, like the related mountain voles, who are solitary and promiscuous, have far weaker oxytocin systems. Reptiles have no oxytocin system at all. (1)

"Humans" with sociopathic, hard-core narcissistic, and what Scott Peck calls evil personalities (see People of the Lie), have only small, twisted fragments of an oxytocin system, which are used to manipulate and exploit others. In their minds, everyone else is like them, which justifies their behavior. Their horrifying emptiness is experienced, at a conscious level, as boredom, restlessness, and contempt.

It is unfair to reptiles to call these deranged individuals reptilian. No, reptiles can't empathize or love, but they too are God's beings, intended to be here. Their drives are normal and related to real needs, not malignant and insatiable. The malignant character structures mentioned here are somewhat like deranged reptiles, except with **human** surface-level functional intelligence. The most dangerous among them have near-genius intelligence, and access to wealth. It is fairly obvious that the global capitalist oligarchy contains many of these horrifying shells of humans. There are, I'm sure, numerous individual exceptions to at least some degree (2). And an increasingly inhuman existence awaits us the longer we allow this oligarchy, with its increasingly dangerous technology, and our own internalization of its sick values, to stay in power.

(1) A General Theory of Love; Lewis, Amini, and Lannon, 2000

(2) And now, for the much-ballyhooed gracious charity of the well-heeled ... "Ahh, yeees ... ". For starters, S.F. Bay Area tax filers with incomes STARTING at $200,000 a year in 2012 gave all of 2.8% of their incomes to charity (and this is a tax write-off no less) (S.F. Chronicle, 10-7-14, from Chronicle of Philanthropy). There are a few well-publicized exceptions, but even these need to be looked at. Most "charitable" foundations are largely frauds – designed for show, $$$-making opportunities, better training for all the little workers who create their vast wealth, and control over the Bad (i.e. profit-impairing) Behavior of all those "ignorant", "backward" working people. The individuals behind these "charities" have vastly more wealth than they know what to do with. I could name names, but if this book ever crosses their radar, I will be sued with

their vast wealth. We should also remember that the vicious robber-barons of the 1st Guilded Age (we are now in the 2nd) loved to set up "charitable foundations" too.

See Disordered Personalities at Work; Belinda Board and Katarina Fritzon, Psychology, Crime, and Law, March 2005. They also cite Blackburn, 1988; Babiak, 1995, 1996; Lilienfeld, 1998; Lynam et al, 1999. Also: Successful and Unsuccessful Psychopaths: A Neurological Model, Behavioral Sciences and the Law, Vol. 28, Issue 2, pg. 194-210. A quote from this is **telling**: "There is a very large literature on the important role of psychopathy in the criminal justice system. We know much less about corporate psychopathy and its implications, in large part because of the difficulty in obtaining the active cooperation of business organizations."

My commentary: Personality studies of individuals born into wealth would also be revealing, but would be at least as difficult to conduct. As with research of this kind on top corporate management, the capitalist oligarchy **already knows** what the findings will be, and does **not** want them known. Even this assumes the subjects aren't able to lie on personality tests. Rorscharct ink-blot tests would be more revealing.

The vast, insatiable greed and power-hunger of these individuals is not only completely unknown in normal (hunter-gatherer-permaculturist) human societies, it is also completely unknown in any animals (including reptiles) found in nature. It is a starkly unnatural and depraved condition.

Back to the much ballyhooed gracious charity of the wealthy: "Konczal notes that our social insurance and welfare programs arose precisely because private charity **utterly failed** during the Great Depression." (Mike Konczal, in the journal Democracy, cited by E.J. Dionne Jr., S.F. Chronicle,

3-24-14) Much more recently, charitable contributions fell 7% in 2008, and an additional 6.2% in 2009, when core unemployment hit 10%. (same article) Even then, only **one third** of charitable contributions actually go to the poor. (Center for Philanthropy, Indiana U., cited in same article)

Death Panels for Capitalism!

We have all heard about those alleged nefarious Death Panels that Obamacare will bring.

WHERE are the Death Panels we really need?

You can start a Death Panel in your very community or workplace. Emancipating ourselves is not a spectator sport. Some suggestions (most of which have already been starting):

1. Dealing with bosses and landlords collectively in our daily lives, while preparing to git rid of them altogether. There are worker associations, like Our Walmart, but like official unions, their aims are very limited so far.

2. Study groups/incubators for worker-owned/self-managed enterprises. Tours of existing ones.

3. Use of eminent domain to end the underwater mortgage/foreclosure crisis – i.e. Richmond, CA.

4. Medical billing defense: forcing full transparency on the U.S. Healthcare Fraud and Extortion Racket (SEE Time Magazine expose, 3-4-13). Negotiating collectively, from a position of strength/knowledge, over premiums as well as bills. No taxpayer subsidies for fraud and extortion. Learning medicinal food, plants, and preventative lifestyle/care.

5. Neighborhood cooperative childcare, allo-parenting, and mentoring.

6. Community gardens and bulk buying co-ops.

7. Unlearning learned helplessness and spiritually dead/addictive "values". Stop enabling your own enslavement.

8. Rewilding retreats: re-learning the Land, natural skills; group and individual LSD sessions, Scripture study, meditation. Rewilding exposure is especially critical for kids (OMIT the LSD sessions).

9. Extended family and commune formation.

10. Brainstorming, study, and training for mass non-obedience to the global capitalist oligarchy, as well as smaller acts of non-obedience. Git fluid and unpredictable! And humorous – if the Official Left manages to bore all the working people to death (should anyone be paying attention), WHO will our dear capitalist friends have left to SUCK on?

Christopher Lasch would have called these communities of competence. A growing decentralized network of community-based affinity groups will be more difficult for the Political Police to infiltrate and destroy. Centralized Officious Movements and Pretentious Vanguard Parties have already been tried too many times. The Snowden NSA leak should remind us that the above list clearly constitute Terrorist Activities. Why this very book is clearly a Terrorist Indoctrination and Training Manual!

The bankruptcy of elitist liberalism

REPLY TO DEBRA SAUNDERS EDITORIAL: "Healthy, middle-aged, and over-squeezed thanks to Obamacare".

I agree with your 10-10-13 editorial about Obamacare – see my attached commentary on a similar article. You are careful: "Probably these readers represent a very small but very vocal minority." I don't have any facts (yet), but I doubt this minority is very small. I don't care that what is being done to these people isn't being done to me, or that I stand to benefit from it. It's just plain wrong.

Obamacare is Exhibit A of what liberalism does very well: re-arrange the unfairness imposed on working people while barely touching the root of ugly problems that don't need to exist in the first place.

Elitist liberalism has graced working people with serious regressive taxes (Social Security, Medicare), pitted working people against each other with "affirmative action" quotas and forced busing, done everything it can to gut the 2nd Amendment ("We caun't let THOSE people have their guns."), and endlessly cooks up authoritarian social-engineering schemes to "correct" the bad behavior of "ignorant, backward" working people (especially rednecks – i.e. those of us of Scots-Irish decent, elitist liberals favorite whipping-boy). Then, just to show how "progressive" it is, liberalism will TORMENT the very wealthy with some "terrifying" (to quote a Wall St. banker) 1% tax increase on their vast income. Which they will then proceed to evade. And so (Surprise! Surprise!), white male working-class people are now the hardest constituency of the Right, more so even than the wealthy. Small wonder that very, very wealthy individuals like Soros are more than happy to shower liberal politicians with plenty of $$$.

I'm not a conservative. I'm in fact an anarchist. When enough working people throw off all the learned helplessness this degenerate society does everything to encourage, and attain self-management capacity, coupled with DIRECT ownership and control over wealth creation, it will create the practical basis for a radical reduction of government that will make Reagan look like a Kennedy liberal.

Also, I loved your "Farming Babies is Unfair" editorial. Conservatives aren't expected to be concerned about gross unfairness imposed on poor women. Maybe you get it because you are a woman. The bad culture you refer to has a name. It is called Late Capitalism.

What's in a word? "Radical"

RADICAL (from merriam-webster.com)

1. Of, relating to, or proceeding from a root
2. Of, or relating to the origin: FUNDAMENTAL
3. Very different from the usual or traditional: EXTREME
4. Slang: EXCELLENT, COOL

From Latin radicalis, from earlier radic-, radix "root"

NEVER MIND Webster's Dictionary, which anyone can quickly consult. Most Americans automatically assume "radical" means extreme or violent. Nearly ALL journalists in the capitalist media assume this, and I doubt this is some deliberate Nefarious Conspiracy to make real radicals look bad. It is an embedded assumption, made without even thinking.

Then, of course, there are the much-harped-on "Radical Islamists", i.e. terrorists. Here the word "radical" is stretched beyond recognition to mean the mass killers of civilians. What "radicalized" the Boston killers? the capitalist media repeatedly asks.

If there is anyone who could be legitimately called radical Muslims, it is the Sufis, who are very interested in "mysticism", i.e. Direct Knowledge. It is worth noting here that the Taliban in Pakistan are starting to kill Sufis.

Direct Knowledge, proceeding from a direct, unmediated relationship with the inmost, final Reality that all creation and life emanates from, is going to the final Root. It is the Final Radicalism.

From this proceeds the capacity for enduring fundamental individual and social change.

Radicalism in the U.S.A.

"Blessed are they who expect nothing, for they shall not be disappointed."
- George Orwell

That old Beatles song: "Revolution"

A relic from 1968, this odious, dishonest song still manages to get lots of airplay on 2 of the 3 rock stations I listen to, 45 years later.

Most readers of this book will be too young to remember a time when millions of Americans actually believed radical change was a real possibility here. I was only a child, aged 10 to 15, but I've never seen hope remotely approaching that since.

". . . we-ell you know, we all want to change the world." Deliberate dishonesty, no commentary needed.

"You tell me it's the institution, we-ell you know, you've got to free your mind instead." A false dichotomy, and more deliberate dishonesty you would expect from very, very wealthy rock stars. It is very easy to "free your mind" (false in their case) and "create your own reality" (i.e. create an external reality organized around your own narcissistic disorder) when you are very, very wealthy.

"But if you talk about destru-u-ction, well you know that you can count me out." The only destruction they are concerned with here is any that entails their vast fortunes. And any "revolution" that needs to curry the favor of very, very wealthy rock stars is a pathetic excuse for a "revolution" indeed.

It should be noted here that our dear friends in the global capitalist oligarchy are very fond of something they like to call "creative destruction". Destruction is "creative" when it serves the capitalist's vast, insatiable greed; never mind if the lives of millions of working people are ground and crushed in the process. To the class enemy, the vast, horrifying slums of Dubai and Mumbai, with lots of shit running in their very hot, narrow streets, are "creative"(1).

A conservative UN accounting in 2005 is that more than 1 billion people worldwide are condemned to these capitalist Gulags. (2)

How different modernization works when it is under worker's control, **we** control its effects on **us**, and get **all** the productivity gains. More wealth for us created with less work and far less drudgery? What's not to like? When workers call the shots, we modernize the productive base much more quickly and efficiently than capitalists do, as proven in Catalonia in 1936, and Mondragon since its inception.

In the years ahead, modernization will by necessity mean creating a higher **quality** of life with radically less resource consumption and ecosystem degradation. (This will need to be coupled with a continued and spreading birth rate well below the replacement rate, to reduce overpopulation. We can thank the growing emancipation of women for this.)

More generally, I use the word destruction in this book in context, and without apology.

"But if you go carrying pictures of Chairman Mao, it ain't gonna make it with anyone any-how." Here the Beatles were dead on. Mao was a monster with the blood of millions of innocent people on his hands, the majority from the mass starvation inflicted by "The Great Leap Forward" in the late 1950's. Mao has been thankfully flushed down the toilet of history where he belongs.

A FORWARD ON DAMAGED HUMANS

It is childish to expect that people who have grown up in a sick society will suddenly become well when they embrace a radical political ideology.

"Damaged humans" also needs some serious qualifying here. The damage is a continuum. And what is generally true breaks down a lot at an individual level.

Given what a mess we live in, very significant numbers of surprisingly healthy individuals can be found in it. You may hear about them doing community service or mentoring, or may even know them personally. Growing up in unusually healthy families, they naturally attract the healthiest people into their lives. They are neither greedy, status-seeking, nor lazy. They grow up to be stable, skilled, creative, and good problem solvers; they actually settle down with one partner who they love, and are good parents. They are, in short, able to create better lives than the lot of most people here.

Their downfall can be naivite. They can assume the larger society is mostly as healthy and well-meaning as they and their family/friends are, making them vulnerable to the vast minefield of capitalist traps the system has waiting for us (these have been discussed elsewhere). These people are usually not highly political, either Left or Right. They also tend not to see the traps and sickness they do encounter as socially systemic. As a result, the one **huge** trap most fall into is having kids before they are free from capitalism. Few Americans have this freedom, and attaining it takes time and a sustained will for those who can even see to do it (unless you are born into money). If you have kids to provide for, and are stuck with a boss, a grinding and intrusive work-load, a bone-crushing mortgage, and a nasty commute, you are **trapped**. (And the capitalists, of course, know this.) It is truly amazing that anyone in a life-trap like this can be a decent parent. A social solution is necessary.

Unfortunately for real societal problem-solving, political radicalism, when it is as marginal as it is now, tends to attract the most damaged people of an already sick society. There are numerous exceptions. The non-exceptions see their own personal torment reflected in the larger sick society. And this is **no** delusion. A sick society reproduces itself in the sick character structures of individuals. I was **no** exception in my youth. I only became one after a **lot** of messy, painful internal work, which I never could have done without a very deep spiritual foundation. With raw, stark insight from large doses of LSD, I decided to get as radical with **myself** as I would with the larger society. (This was from 1984 to 1988. With **no** prospects for radical social change, my timing was good.) The reward has been deep and lasting.

I have to credit the one-dimensional political/economic radicalism of my pre-LSD youth for one big advantage. I had **no** illusions about what kind of society I was living in, **acted** accordingly, and this has served me **very** well.

U.S. radicalism now

With the temporary exception of the Occupy movement in the Fall of 2011, there has been no mass radical movement in the U.S. since the early 1970's.

At its peak, the Occupy movement had the sympathy of 55% of the American people. Even after a lot of bad press made possible by Occupy's lack of logistical preparation, Occupy still had the sympathy of 45%. By contrast, the Tea Party movement peaked in the Fall of 2010 with 30% sympathizing; this has since shrunk to 20%. And this is despite, very unlike Occupy, being **very** well funded by right-wing capitalist oligarchs.

What is striking about this is that Occupy was a spontaneous mass revulsion at the entire capitalist system itself. I have never seen anything like it here in my life. A qualifier: many moderate sympathizers (and even some participants) would say things like: "I'm not against capitalism. I just want it to work for everybody." (a sad oxymoronic fantasy). What is also striking is that in the one major recent poll (Pew Research, released 12-28-11) that asks this question, 40% of Americans respond **negatively** to the word "capitalism" (50% respond positively).

The entire system itself is moving into a mass crisis of legitimacy. This could get real interesting if people decide they've finally had enough and actually **do** something.

So where are America's active radicals now?

Before and since Occupy, active U.S. radicalism has been a very small scene, mostly working on single issues and in-group polemics. If you have not been exposed to it, do not have high expectations. This is not likely to be a problem, since radicals have an image problem in the U.S.

Outside the single-issue groups, the most visible groups are the numerous small, hard-line ideological groups usually referred to (accurately) as sectarian groups. Their internal life ranges from authoritarian to totalitarian, and they are only interested in building their own little group. Any involvement in broader or potentially broader organizations is mostly to serve this end, and they have a well-deserved bad reputation among the much larger number of radical activists who are not members of any of these groups. The majority of these groups are Trotskyist, but many are Maoist.

There is a much larger number of small, usually locally-based anarchist grouplets. Some of these, like the group that initiated the Occupy the Farm action (Spring 2012) on U.C.-owned land in Albany, CA, are innovative, skilled, even brilliant. (Occupy the Farm distributed an entire ton of organic produce they had grown to the surrounding working-class community.) Many others can be as bad as the Trotskyist and Maoist sects, with even less tactical sense. The U.S. anarchist scene is in general very ingrown, and riven with petty personal conflicts. Also, many self-described anarchists are "scenesters", into punk rock and not much else (see "fashion anarchism", also called "radical chic" when it goes big).

The Trotskyist and Maoist sects have **no** future in America. **Nobody** in America is interested in a State-Owned and Centrally Planned Economy run by a Glorious Vanguard Party. Sadly, most of the anarchist grouplets don't have much more of a future. But the more innovative, practical, and reality-based anarchist projects **do**. America should be fertile ground for anarchism. If de-facto anarchism does become a serious force here, it may get called something like "Left Libertarianism", since anarchism is strongly associated with chaos and violence in most people's minds.

More generally, U.S. radical activism is gripped with a not-fully-conscious sense of futility. Nothing can be done, it seems, to broadly impact the larger society in a lasting way, or even radically change our own lives. Our small numbers hardly help any. One of the unpleasant and wasteful results of this is infighting (At least we can impact **each other**!).

Really this is not very different than the not-fully-conscious sense of helplessness that pervades American working people as a whole. People don't like where things are at, far less where they are going. But no one seems to know what to **do** about it, and (preconsciously) fear it wouldn't make any difference if they did. A big part of this is circular, as in vicious cycle: if enough people **did** know what to do, and **did** it, it **would** matter. That would break the vicious cycle.

Occupy temporarily broke through. But when its tactical rigidity was defeated, no one knew what to do. So everybody went home, back to the daily grind.

I **have** radically changed my life. And it is the aim of this entire book to help **end** our learned helplessness. Our **own** learned helplessness is the single most powerful weapon in the hands of those who would enslave us. **We can end it**, and the cost of not doing so will only grow worse.

(1) "Economists have tended to accentuate the good side of slums." (The Economist, 2-8-14, pg.72) I'll spare you the rest, and this article means slums like those of Dubai, which is also a favorite offshore banking haven for the ill-gotten gains of the global capitalist oligarchy. No doubt these sociopath economists have never spent any actual time in one of these slums, far less "lived" in one for any extended period of time.

(2) Planet of Slums, Mike Davis, pg. 23

What is anarchism?
What is the Left?

What curious times we live in. Here in America, the Hard Right in Congress is now being called "anarchist" and "radical".

Real anarchists, including most anarchists who identify as Left, are completely outside the tired more government vs. more capitalism binary that most people understand as Left vs. Right. Never mind that you can have more of **both** – i.e. Hitler or Pinochet.

The progressive/social-democrat vision is a big, benevolent Nanny-State that takes care of everybody. The anarchist vision is direct self-management and **no** State. They couldn't be farther apart, though I think most ordinary progressives mean well. Progressives just lack depth and vision. Marxists would claim to have the anarchist vision too, but for most of them, only **after** the State takes over everything. This is beyond tortured logic.

Socialist-feminism and anarcha-feminism are redundancies. There can't be **any** serious anarchist or socialist theory without radical feminism being central to its very core. This should be obvious and non-controversial. Patriarchy was the **first** class society.

Feminism, including radical feminism, gained wide traction so fast in the 1970's because there is a species-memory (called the collective unconscious by Carl Jung) of the nearly 2 million years that normal humans had gender equality. Patriarchy only showed up, as a radical degeneration (and throw-back to the upright apes), 10,000 years ago in a few parts of the world. .

American fascism will have distinctly American characteristics. It will be "libertarian". Attempts at vicious repression will largely be conducted by the private sector (it's **so** much more efficient) – privately hired thugs, mercenaries, and death squads. The U.S. **does** also have a huge police-state apparatus. **Thank God** so many ordinary Americans own "assault rifles" (i.e. serious combat firepower). We can defend ourselves, with something better than pop-guns.

As for the green anarchist vision – fully normal/wild humans who have what are now called "mystical experiences" all the time – **that** is beyond what almost anyone would understand as politics or economics. But it has radical political/economic implications. Fundamental obstructions to the full emancipation of humans need to be removed.

And now, a Politically Correct Leftist Critique of anarchism: "Self-education, self-organization, self-reliance/do-it-yourselves (DIY), self-management, self-enlightenment, self-emancipation, self-defense . . . self, self, SELF! ALL you anarchists care about is YOURSELVES!" Well? Who **else** is gonna git the job done? Government/the State is a special interest group, with an inherent agenda of its own. And no, it is **not** your emancipation.

What is work?

In an essay Bob Black wrote, titled The Abolition of Work, he said something like this: When creation is reduced to production, recreation is reduced to convolesence. Dead on.

But is work inherently forced productivity, alienated labor, under conditions of economic slavery/exploitation? I'd provisionally define work as anything requiring effort that contributes to the well-being of others. This is a different definition than Bob Black's. Normal (hunter-gatherer-permaculturist) humans spend 15-20 hours a week providing for their material needs. All other waking hours are devoted to play and direct (usually collective) communion with Reality. But normal humans don't have anything like our split between "work" and "play", let alone the frenzied, intrusive (thanks to techie crap), grinding overwork we have now. Nearly one-third of American workers get 6 hours of sleep or less a night (CDC, cited in The Economist, 8-17-13, pg.58). It should be noted here that sleep deprivation is used by cults to control people, and causes brain damage in children.

For 29 years, I've earned a living designing, planting/installing, and maintaining beautiful gardens. This improves other people's quality of life. Many of my clients have become personal friends. When I was a kid, it was a hobby. It was play. I'm still not tired of it, and at age 56, have no interest in retirement.

When this book happened, I never set out to write a book. I read voraciously, for the pure, intrinsic pleasure of it. And I write when stuff comes to me, for the pure, intrinsic pleasure of doing it. This book wrote itself. I **never** turn writing into a job – like "It is now time to sit down and write." far less with bosses and imposed deadlines. I never would have written a **thing** if I allowed **that** crap in my life. When stuff comes to me, I just set everything else aside and git it down.

The freeing up of normal human creativity will require the destruction of economic slavery, exploitation, and finally anything we now understand as a job. This will require healing the damaged/deranged brain development resulting from growing up and living under Late Capitalism. (Steve Mithen posits that Neanderthals, and Sapiens before 40,000 years ago, had a vastly more developed musical capacity, just with their voices, than humans alive today. But alas! Music doesn't fossilize.)

I have lived through a long period where there was almost no social possibility of emancipation here in America. I had to do it on my own, and I did. (Rednecks are like that.) I have **no** government safety net. No unemployment insurance (the vast housing crash here in California hurt my landscaping business), no worker's comp or disability insurance (control over my work, and a lot of control over how much I work, makes this far less necessary), no health insurance (an ounce of prevention is worth a ton of cure – particularly here in the U.S.A.), no Medicare/Medical (1), no Social Security income, no SSI, no welfare, no food stamps, no subsidized housing. The only thing I depend on govt. for is the infrasctructure I drive to work on. And I pay taxes.

But I have adequate financial security. (A California state law, passed in 2006, prevents hospitals from stripping me clean should I suffer a catastrophic event. My income is under 350% of the federal poverty line.) What I did was this: systematically destroy over time (or pre-emptively prevent) every ability of the capitalist system to suck on the wealth I create – bosses, landlords, bone-crushing mortgages, student loans, credit card debt, and finally, the U.S. Healthcare Fraud and Extortion Racket (SEE Time magazine expose, 3-4-13).

I've had a little personal exposure to the wealthy. Their sense of entitlement is so grotesquely bloated that most Americans could scarcely even imagine it. Blinded by their material wealth, seclusion, and ideology, they can scarcely imagine what working people are capable of. Let alone what most of us are "living" under now. This blindness will not save them. It will help enable the destruction of their rule.

(1) Postscript: In 2014, I qualified for Medical under the new expansion. This will end if my book does well.

THE RED PANTHER
REDNECK PROVISIONAL PROGRAM

COUGAR KITTY WANTS YOU!

1. What are the chains we aim to destroy? These: bosses, rent gouging, bone-crushing mortgages, endless crawling commutes, taxation of honest work instead of blood-sucking, 40 to 60 hours a week of wage/salary slavery in cubicles and factories – in large part a result of our being pitted against global slave labor havens, the destruction of our Land; malignant, cold-blooded rat-race "values" – greed, conceit, power-hunger, dishonesty/manipulation; and finally, the crushing runaway cost of all the disease this sickness breeds, "treated" by the U.S. Healthcare Fraud and Extortion Racket.

We are not interested in putting a "happier" face on these abominations. We aim to completely destroy capitalist rule and all class society. This is the necessary precondition for the emancipation of humans.

2. We want Eden back. We love the back woods for good reason. The Land must be returned to the People so that the People can return to God. This will require the direct expropriation of logging corporations, railroads, utilities, mining corporations, big agribusiness, wealthy individuals, and the (capitalist) State. **None** of these oligarchs created the Land – God did. Nearly all "white" people own **no** land, or only a debt-loaded pitiful crumb (**who** can live decently on a tiny city lot?). Humans need wild space to be happy. Humans of European ancestry only have a sickly whitish pallor when imprisoned in factories or office cubicles. We are normally (when free to live like normal humans) a tawny color (like a panther), only more red. That's why were called rednecks. We too are "people of color". All normal humans are. The black belt needs to be returned to the African Diaspora that was enslaved on it (Remember the 40 acres and a mule that never showed up?). Redneck Land needs to be

94

returned to the rednecks. Real, rather than token, repatriation of Land needs to be made to the Original People ("Indians").

3. External freedom is of little use to those who are not internally free. A **direct** (un-mediated, experiential) relationship with God (the inmost, final Reality that all life emanates from) is the foundation of true freedom. When you **experience** what was intended for us, you will understand the depth and magnitude of what has been taken from us. You can't take anyone else's word for it (it **can't** be put into words) – **you have to see for yourself**.

4. We are not interested in squabbling with other subtribes of that vast supertribe that is the working class over what crumbs the capitalist oligarchy will throw us. Any crumb we get will be gouged out of other working people under the present system. This is a **waste** of our time and everyone else's. When capitalist rule is destroyed, working people can haggle over the **whole** "pie". Maybe then all of us can be more generous with each other. And with spiritual discernment, we can see what parts of the "pie" simply need to be destroyed. Our job is this: what can our subtribe contribute to the emancipation of **all** working people? Rednecks have a lot to bring: our toughness, our self-reliance/resourcefulness, our fighting ability/combat experience, our firepower, our intimacy with the Land, for many of us – a deep spiritual life, and especially where this is present - the capacity for fearlessness. There are tens of millions of rednecks. If we put our minds to it, we could destroy capitalist rule all by ourselves. Imagine what we could do allied with Blacks, Latinos and other working-class subtribes!

5. We want ownership/power **directly** in the hands of working people. And to enable this, our defense of the 2nd Amendment (without which all the rest of the Bill of Rights would be toilet paper) will

be without compromise. Our hatred for capitalist rule should **never** be confused with support for what has been called "Communism". What Is to Be Done?, by V.I. Lenin (1903), is the founding document of modern "Communism". Lenin, a child of the well-to-do, claimed that working people could never advance beyond "narrow trade union consciousness" on our own. Fundamental change could only happen if we were led by a centralized Party of university-educated cadre implanted among our People by our "betters". He even called them "Professional Revolutionaries". Do we really need to be ruled by "red" yuppies? The "Communist" Party is a career ladder. We can see the **results** of this anti-working class ideology: the monstrous crimes of Stalin and Mao; and now – "People's China" is the favorite slave-labor haven of the global capitalist oligarchy(*) – enabled by the "Communist" Party elite looting the "People's State" and becoming private capitalists. **No one** should be surprised by any of this. And all of this needs to be smashed. If we are sympathetic to any "foreign" ideology, it is anarchism – as practiced by the workers and farmers of Spain in 1936-1937. This was the farthest advance of working-class power/ freedom the modern world has ever seen. See Anthony Beevor's The Battle for Spain (1982), and George Orwell's Homage to Catalonia to start with. These people were a lot like rednecks. All that being said, Lenin also wrote some useful works, like State and Revolution (1917). And there are people who consider themselves Leninists who have contributed greatly to the emancipation of our People.

(*) UPDATE, 12-21-13, around 4 years after this chapter was originally written: Thanks to the unruly, cantankerous behavior of Chinese workers, China is no longer the slave labor haven it once was. Median wages have quadrupled since 2000, tho I don't think this is inflation-adjusted. Chinese inflation has been moderate – 2% to 5% per year. Capitalists in China have already started to offshore jobs from China to new slave-labor havens, but alas!, these new havens lack China's educated workforce and good infrastructure. It must be **hard** being a global capitalist. My heart bleeds.

Redneck economic data
All from Born Fighting, by James Webb 2004

A survey of 8 sample counties in Tennessee in 1850 "showed that more than half of all adult males (free and slave together) owned no land at all." (pg. 180)

And even as late as 1983, "the top 1% of landowners possessed half the land in Appalachia, the top 5% owned nearly two-thirds." (pg. 181)

Regionwide, less than 5% of the whites in the South owned slaves, 53% of them 5 slaves or fewer. (pg. 212)

Page 216 – economic facts just prior to Civil War

"An actual majority of farmers in the South did not own their own land, instead having to operate as tenant farmers or sharecroppers. Tenant farmers averaged $73 for a year's work, sharecroppers from $38 to $87, depending on the state (1937). In 1937, the average income in the South was only $314, while the rest of the country averaged $604.

Of the 1,831,000 tenant families in the region, about 66% were white (the South's population at this time was 71% white). Approximately half of the sharecroppers were white, living under conditions almost identical with those of black sharecroppers. In 1937, the 13 Southern states had 36 million individuals." (pg. 269)

"Family income, in the 1974 NORC study, varied by almost $5000, from a Jewish high of $13,340 to the (white) Baptist low of $8693. By comparison, in the 1970 census, the variance in family income between whites taken as a whole and blacks was only $3600.

... white Baptists averaged only 10.7 years of education . . .at the same level of black Americans in 1970." (pg. 324)

After the Civil War ended, reconstruction was a boon mostly to the Northern industrialist oligarchy. The Southern landed oligarchy continued to suck on their "freed" black slaves, who were merely converted to tenant farmers, sharecroppers, and agricultural laborers, the same condition about half of Southern rednecks were already living under.

Nearly 150 years after the Civil War ended, the scions of the slave-owning oligarchy still have their $$$, and blacks have still not been repatriated the 40 acres and a mule they were promised long ago (or its modern equivalent in productive assets). As elitist liberals and Politically Correct "radical" Identity Politicians would have it, rednecks are to blame for all this, and by extension, all working-class whites. Which is why we, of course, **not** the wealthy oligarchy, **must** pay for any redress of injustice to blacks.

Tribalism and racism

"We just **can't** have a redneck chapter without a discussion of racism, **can** we now." (deliver in a Jimi Hendrix voice). The words "redneck" and "racist" mean the same thing in most people's minds, needless to say. It is unfair to stereotype **all** rednecks this way, but it is sadly true for the majority of us.

If the sad truth be told, **most** people are racist to some degree. Studies show that whites in general, and right-wing whites in particular, are the least honest about their own racism. Everyone knows about coded racism. Blacks are actually **more** willing than whites to say blacks are more racist than whites (1). Most whites **do not** like to talk about racism, and young whites have made sadly little progress on this (2).

There is, unfortunately, a big, nasty fly in the ointment of the human Deep Structure. Humans did not evolve to have loyalty to humans as a species. We evolved to have loyalty to our band and tribe. This was the group natural selection that enabled humans to happen in the first place. Tribal identity most easily fixates along ethnic or racial lines.

This is why racism/nationalism is so intractable. Instead of "Workers of the world, unite!", Europe got 2 unimaginably vicious world wars, resulting in the extermination of tens of millions of people. And that was just the European tribes fighting each other. Never mind the genocide and slavery of colonialism, or the recent genocide between two big African tribes in overcrowded Rwanda.

Tribal wars were much less frequent, and **vastly** less destructive before the Fall, but they did occur. (Normal humans, having a deep spiritual life, and lacking the idolatry of religion, **never** had religious wars.)

Racism is so deeply embedded that studies have shown when people are shown the face of someone who is racially different (especially a male), a fear response is immediately triggered in the limbic system before the conscious mind can even process it.

This fear reflex is in most people quickly overridden when the racially different person is put in context, say a doctor or a teacher (3). Racism can also be at least partially overridden by growing up in a multi-racial neighborhood from a very young age, like I did. Tribe then fixates on some other unifying factor, such as being working-class or American, like it did in my case.

The above paragraph should be cause for hope, and intent, because racism is the biggest single obstruction to the emancipation of working people. I have **no** illusions about Obama (or Obamacare), but the heavy racial polarization of the 2012 election should make the problem obvious.

Few among the capitalist oligarchy want to bring Hitler back. But if they get desperate enough, who knows? What would an American Hitler look like? For starters, we can be certain it will be draped in the star-spangled banner.

The Tea Party set claim to love America. But for most of them, "America" does **not** include you unless you are straight, white, and conservative. Should anyone wonder what the racial politics of the Tea Party are, it is worth noting that 80% were satisfied with the Zimmerman verdict, compared to 49% of whites as a whole, and all of 5% of blacks (2). For most of the Tea Party, "America" is code for only the shrinking minority of Americans who are just like them, and soon, a proto-fascist agenda.

Footnotes

1.   Rasmussen poll, July 1-2, 2013, 1000 adults

2.   Pew Research poll, July 17-21, 1480 adults

3.   Newsweek, 9-4-09, has a lot of similar data, but not these particular studies. I remember the results, but not the source. The Newsweek article cited here has some good advice, drawn from practice, on how to deal with race issues with small children. It also notes how even liberal white parents squirm at talking plainly and directly about race with their kids. (White parents who are committed racists, however, do **not**.)

Theses on Human Emancipation
(to git all pretentious)

ONE

We have to be class war anarchists because ONLY the working class has the social weight necessary to destroy capitalist hegemony (the current form of economic/spiritual slavery)

We have to be green anarchists because:

1. Industrial civilization is unsustainable.
2. The destruction of class society CANNOT be consolidated until the Deep Structure of normal human nature is fully regenerated.

TWO

The emancipation of working people as a whole has 3 broad fronts:

1. Class war inside the capitalist sector: worker self-organization, strikes, especially irregular/unpredictable strikes, sit-down strikes/ occupations; rent strikes, mortgage strikes; shutting down Wall St., K St. and other nerve centers of the global capitalist oligarchy with mass, sustained civil disobedience. On a pettier level – employee theft and sabotage (it creates attrition for the class enemy).
2. The growth, diversification, and vertical integration of the worker-owned/self-managed sector. This develops the functional capacity for working-class rule.
3. The Return. People who have taken up the complete regeneration of the original Deep Structure of human nature. This means rewilding in the back woods. The generation that takes up the Return is too damaged to fully enter the Promised Land. This will be for our

Grandchildren. The sanctuaries of the Return will serve as retreats for our people still inside the cities taking up the first 2 fronts.

The emancipation of women . . .

I'm not qualified here to say what women should do, being a guy and all . . . Worse still, my brain masculinization is well within male-typical range, and I had deep male bonding during the critical effect period for the formation of this in childhood.

The emancipation of oppressed nationalities . . .

Except for rednecks, I'm not qualified to say much here either. Except that it is self-defeating for "white" working people to obstruct the emancipation of working people "of color".

The end of homophobia . . .

I'm not trying to run Politically Correct Affirmative Action Quotas here. This is personal, and I've discussed my private life very little in this book. More in a separate chapter – Love relations during the Emancipation.

Trapped in a Transitional Stage!

Transitional Economics:
WHERE WORKING PEOPLE ARE TAKING POWER NOW

(written in 1997, updated 1998-2000)

POSTSCRIPT, 2013

When this was written, I wasn't interested in dreaming up airy "Imagine" theories. I had been studying ACTUALLY EXISTING examples of wealth creation owned and managed by working people, including in the area where I lived. These have already grown since this was written.

This is something like Adam Smith's description of early capitalism in his Wealth of Nations (1776). My work here is somewhat dated, but the basic principles remain in operation.

Back in the 1990's, I had never heard of Green Anarchism or John Zerzan. So this work is confined to the logic of industrial/"post" industrial civilization. Which is why it is subtitled "Trapped in a Transitional Stage!". But there is a very practical link here: How are we going to come up with the $$$ to git Land for rewilding sanctuaries if we let exploiters TAKE the wealth we create?

A note on sources. I have not footnoted all the facts I lay out here on existing worker-owned/self-managed enterprises. They are drawn from the attached bibliography at the end of this chapter, and what I have heard directly from members of these firms where I live.

ORIGINAL ESSAY

Back in the days when heavy industry and mass assembly line production of standardized products were first developing, capital was massing into ever larger blocs at the point of production. Growing economy of scale was the key to success. Workers were herded into ever larger factories and most workers were de-skilled.

This peaked in the Fordist/Taylorist period (1920 - 1970) and fit the predictions of Marx. This was to end in the organization of capital into one final vast bloc owned by the State. Society would become one immense planned factory ("scientific socialism").

Supposedly this was to occur under the political supremacy of working people (or the "toiling masses" as the Statists liked to call us). What we actually got was Nazism (overtly right-wing Statism or "National Socialism") in economically advanced Germany, and pseudo-leftist Stalinism ("International Socialism") in economically backwards Russia. These were not accidents of history.

(By the 1930's, capitalism had made such a mess that even the capitalists were discovering the virtues of Statism. Hitler promised the German industrialists and bankers he would crush all independent labor unions - a promise he kept.)

When farmers and artisans were first herded into factories, de-skilled, and enslaved, many were attracted to direct self-management under direct worker-ownership as a way out - the co-operative commonwealth of the U.S. Knights of Labor and the European mutualists/anarchists.

As a hereditary proletariat developed, without any self-management experience, this embryonic vision was lost. The authoritarian nanny-State then became our would-be savior. "Being determines consciousness." (I would say being pre-disposes consciousness.) This also seemed practical, given the huge and growing blocs of capital needed to run production. In the Leninist version, Statism would be led by intellectuals implanted into the labor movement from outside the working class (see What Is To Be Done, V.I. Lenin, 1903).

Lenin also wrote some admirable works, the best of which is State and Revolution (1917), but Leninism also contains the seeds of Stalinism. The monstrous crimes of Stalin were prefigured by the "War Communism" led by Lenin and Trotsky during Russia's civil war.

In practice, totalitarian Statism did prove faster (at a horrible cost) in the early, quantitative buildup of crude heavy industry. This advantage rapidly broke down as the productive base began to differentiate into anything more advanced and complex. The crude, centralized, lumbering State planning machine could not cope with it.

Had the Soviet system been any truly post-capitalist mode of production - even a "degenerated worker's state" - it would have won the cold war. It's productive base would have overtaken the U.S..

Statism in practice has proven to be more like a pre-capitalist mode of wealth creation - a pseudo-modern mutation of Marx's "oriental despotism". It is telling that in its purist form - Stalinism - Statism came to power almost exclusively in economically backward countries. In all exceptions (East Germany, Czecholslovakia), it was imposed from outside.

It was the last reactive gasp of a pre-capitalist age.

Even in its most benign form - social democracy - Statism is proving to be an attempt at post-capitalist aims thru pre-capitalist means. Social democrats almost seemed to sense this at some level - preferring to leave the organization of the productive base itself largely in the hands of the capitalists. Helpful in its early success (1946 - 1972), this is proving to be the undoing of social democracy. It is now being slowly strangled by a low-intensity capital strike, with unemployment in the 10% - 15% range.

With growing globalization, capital has had ever less need to buy social peace in western Europe.

(To the extent that exploiters pay for the social safety net at all, it has been mostly indirect in the form of payroll taxes and limitations on firing workers. Even here, this is only to the extent that they cannot take it out of wages -"indirect labor burden" is an accounting category for this - or pass this cost back to working people as consumers thru higher prices.

The rich, as owners and controllers, have control over how they take their real income. With the rich creating so many - increasingly global - shell games with their income, income taxes fall primarily on skilled workers and workers putting in long hours. By one estimate, half the millionaires in Hamburg, Germany, pay no income taxes at all. The total tax burden on the average German is about 40%.)

A direct State takeover of productive assets is no solution to this problem. The inherent crudeness of such a process would only damage or destroy the finely differentiated, complex, and flexible productive base of an advanced (post)industrial economy - even without any capital strike at all.

(Certain finely crafted forms of State intervention, even if difficult to effectively enforce, can be very useful. An example of this would be a tax on real estate speculation - on housing held as income property only, it would start at 95% of profit on holdings turned over within 2 years, and would fall off progressively with the length of holding before sale. A similar tax on currency speculation would be another, as well as taxes on all other short-term transactions.)

Karl Marx died over 100 years ago. At this stage in the development of the productive base, capitalism, and technology itself, are beginning to set in motion the mode of production that will organically displace/supercede capitalist rule. This will occur in a very different way than Marx predicted.

Capitalism will be increasingly unable to compete with the forces of production created by a growing free working class, with the functional superiority inherent in a free working class. Capitalism will prove inherently unable to duplicate our deep structural advantages, and the market, which it thinks of as its private property, will be the terrain on which its rule is permanently destroyed.

Back to the near past and present. Within the productive base of the advanced capitalist nations, automation and offshoring, increasingly took over the unskilled/semiskilled repetitive tasks of mass production at a lower price than (organized) labor.

At the same time, increasingly flexible, sophisticated, and cheap technology made possible customized, small batch production for ever more finely differentiated market niches. This also gave rise to the need for more skilled services, often "packaged" with the product. In a growing array of markets and market niches, the scale of production began to fall. Less capital was needed to break into a market, or create a new one.

At the same time, growing purchasing power created by the growing productive base generated more demand for services of all kinds, many of them requiring little start-up capital. (Capitalist income distribution concentrated this demand among the upper middle class and rich.)

These trends accelerated thru the 1980's and 1990's.

Between 1991 and 1995, U.S. based firms employing fewer than 100 workers created 9.7 million jobs (net). Firms employing between 100 and 499 workers created 1 million jobs, and firms employing 500 workers or more destroyed 3.2 million jobs (net). (1)

The net growth in sales (real dollars) of the 500 biggest U.S. based corporations between 1992 and 1996 ran at all of 0.7% per year, considerably worse than the 2.2% annual growth rate for the U.S. economy as a whole over the same period. (2)

The widening destruction of market oligopolies, and the demand/ technological capacity for quality and differentiation, forced exploiters to load more responsibility onto increasingly skilled workers - who are closest to the customers and actually create the wealth. At the same time, these capitalists retain control at the top - and with globalization/weaker unions, grind these workers harder and harder for less real pay. (From 1997 to 2000, some real income growth finally began to "trickle down" to the bottom 80%, at least outside places like the Bay Area with its stratospheric housing costs.)

While all this was going on, small but growing numbers of workers have permanently withdrawn their creative power from the capitalists, and created new firms under direct worker ownership and control. Some of these were buy-outs; many others were originally inspired by temporary mass factory occupations - France in 1968 and Italy in 1969.

In France even with its heavily Statist political culture, the number of worker-controlled firms grew from 1270 in 1981 to 13,000 in 1998. Italy, with a more anarchist culture, already had just under 20,000 worker-controlled firms in 1981. (3) (Postscript – 54,200 in 2013, see update later in this chapter.) The growth of this sector, in most advanced (post) industrial countries, far exceeds the growth of the capitalist sector. And it has sustained a 30% higher level of productivity in France and Italy. (4)

The following is a summary of what these property forms look like and how they work.

Socialism, in its true form, can be functionally defined as the working class organized as ruling class. It is a transitional historical stage between capitalism and true communism (classless and stateless society), and contains features of both. Much as mercantilism was a transitional stage between feudalism and capitalism. True socialism will still have property, but without economic slavery, and it will still have exchange, but without exploitation. Those who do the work that creates wealth will have control over their work, and will own/control all the wealth their labor creates. Where worker's control is being successfully created, and is organically displacing capitalism, it is directly by workers themselves and not the State.

ELEMENTS OF SELF-MANAGEMENT
Functional core of working-class rule

OWNERSHIP STRUCTURE Cost of joining firm separated from surplus value accumulated by older workers. Membership is a right to participate and vote – not a salable commodity. (Our freedom is not for sale.) Surplus value accrues to each worker's capital account in proportion to the wealth they create (to each according to their work). Some of the capital (10% - 25%) is indivisible – a permanent investment in the firm's future.

Moderate range of incomes – i.e. no more than 1 to 5 on an hourly basis for our entire sector of the economy – based on skill, physical or mental stress involved, education required, and responsibility. Hiring of non-owners limited to 10% - 25% of total firm workforce (depending on structural flexibility needed for particular market), with strict pay formula to prevent exploitation.

Firms are independent – owned directly by their workers and not the State.

Firms will "rent" capital (paying interest) from credit unions and pension funds, but these lenders will not vote shares.

Note – surplus value, roughly speaking, is the wealth workers create over and above covering living expenses. In addition to enabling the development of our productive base, our total ownership of this surplus value finances disability and retirement payments, without forced and regressive tax collection by the State.

POSTSCRIPT on all this fuss about retirement: When you are doing what you love, are free from bosses and exploitation, aren't working too hard, and have also moved radically towards abolishing the split between "work" and "play" altogether (which normal – i.e. hunter-gatherer-permaculturist – humans don't have to begin with), retirement becomes profoundly uninteresting.

I write this from experience at age 56.

GOVERNING STRUCTURE One worker – one vote. Top management directly elected by workers; little or no middle management. Firms sized to the particular market/market niche they operate in – this usually means 20 – 200 workers. They are loosely linked in federations to gain particular economies of scale where needed, pool experience/expertise, and to form banking and social insurance infrastructures. Major policy decisions in firms and federations are made by direct referendum of workers. Maximum firm autonomy to encourage initiative and innovation from those closest to actual wealth creation and customers – i.e. the workers themselves; also to discourage ugly, wasteful power struggles over a stiflingly and stupidly centralized conglomerate.

DAY-TO-DAY FUNCTIONING Generalized structure: cross-functional, integrated self-managed teams, with authority to commit resources, handle product/service, and work directly with customers, from beginning to end. Application would vary greatly with industry/market-niche/firm in question. All workers have direct access to all the firm's information, as well as information from "outsiders". Cross "training" (skill sharing) to the extent practical. Project leadership rotates, usually as one or another function dominates the process at a particular stage.

(This paragraph is mostly summarized from Liberation Management, by Tom Peters.)

THE INTANGIBLE FACTOR (Psychology) This often shows up on the balance sheets of capitalist or technocratic firms as "goodwill and other intangibles". It can make or break a firm.

In short, it is the character structure / real motives of the individuals in the firm – especially the founders, who set the tone – and the resulting group psychology.

Who shows up to start a firm can be influenced, but not controlled, by firm structure or (claimed) values. Official (claimed) motives may differ greatly from real motives; and the greater the divergence, the more the individuals involved develop a vested interest in denying or being unconscious of what is really going on. This is one central reason why our enterprise federations must be DECENTRALIZED, and new enterprise formation ENCOURAGED. "More at-bats, greater odds of a hit." (Tom Peters)

WORKER-OWNED SECTOR – LEVELS OF CRITICAL MASS

NOTE: The GDP % figures assume we are working 40 hours a week. We would be wise to choose to work less hours, and bring in more worker-owners, which would mean our productivity per hour would be substantially even higher.

1. SUSTAINABLE At present market conditions, a permanent part of the overall economy with a natural tendency to grow. Our sector has already begun to function at a higher level than capitalist firms. Size: maybe 1.5% - 4% of total economy's workforce, and 3% - 10% of GDP.

2. STRATEGIC EQUILIBRIUM Sufficient size, organization, "deep pockets", and flexibility to successfully resist unfair trading practices from still-larger capitalist sector (i.e. collusion, dumping).

Broad popular support for worker-ownership is key here. Size: maybe 5% - 8% of total workforce, 12% - 17% of GDP.

3.   TURNING POINT Sufficient size/organization to permanently displace capitalism as the dominant economic system. Able to create so much opportunity that in time, no one will have to live under capitalism unless they really want to. Given this, and the resulting popular support, any attempt at repression by capitalists would be likely to backfire badly, and would have to be of Nazi proportions to succeed. Size: maybe 10% - 18% of total workforce, 25% - 40% of GDP.

These stages will develop at a varying pace over decades, running parallel to greatly varying levels of class war inside the capitalist sector itself, and in politics /ruling ideas.)

We should remember how long it took free peasants and independent capitalists to finally win out over the feudal and mercantilist oligarchies.

WARNING: (POSTSCRIPT)

The unfair trading practices our sector will face at the beginning of Level 2 are likely to be far worse than collusion or dumping. As a longtime friend put it: "Once the capitalist class decides something is a threat, they will try to crush it." We have already seen this with the Occupy movement. So much for peaceable assembly – guaranteed in our Constitution.

In the case of our enterprises, this will take the form of an ECONOMIC BLOCKADE. Capitalist banks, suppliers, and distributors will refuse to do business with us. (Capitalist banks ALREADY won't lend to us.) This was used to strangle the worker-owned startups formed in association with the Knights of Labor in the 1880's (there were only about 200 of them). It was also used to strangle the black-owned startups associated with the movement led by Marcus Garvey in the early 20th century. So much for "free enterprise".

This is why it is critical for our sector to diversify, develop vertical integration (our own supply chains, distribution, and associated services), and our own banking infrastructure as soon as possible. The Mondragon federation did this.

Broad social awareness of what is going on will also be critical. Workers still inside the capitalist sector can retaliate with strikes and other upheaval, something our sector, where workers are in charge, will be nearly immune to.

The transition from Late Capitalist slavery to a free working class will not be a precious outdoor dining experience. IT WILL BE A PROTRACTED SOCIAL WAR.

Emancipated Labor:
Structural Advantages Over Capitalism

In general: far less inherent conflict of interest within firm. More motivated workers with freed-up creative power.

More specifically:

1. Ability to attract the best workers in a given industry – no comparable capitalist firm can offer the same level of freedom and prosperity to its workers.
2. Freed-up creativity, skill development, and invention; without this being ripped-off by bosses or used against other workers in the firm. The firm can more fully draw upon the abilities of its workers. Jealousies and "office politics" will still have to be dealt with, though within a democratic/decentralized rather than a suck-up hierarchical context.
3. Relatively frictionless flexibility – workers can "do each other's jobs" without being pitted against each other by bosses.
4. ALL productivity gains go to workers – so ability and motivation to improve it is unclouded by a conflict of class interest. Firm federation, plus growth of our sector, makes potential job destruction easier to absorb (in many cases we will just reduce work hours with no cut in pay). Productivity measured against comparable capitalist firms – Washington state plywood firms, 25% - 40% higher; Italian sector as a whole, 33% higher.
5. Lower turnover, less absenteeism, and lower attrition from overt and covert class war within firm: strikes, sabotage, employee theft, workers comp fraud, lawsuits, foot dragging, low morale/resentment/whining.

6. With far more control over our work – lower injury and workers comp rates.

7. Less management overhead – as these functions are to a growing extent directly taken over by workers or eliminated. Greater creativity and efficiency of management – as it is either directly in the hands of workers right at the point of production and closest to customers, or people directly elected by these workers.

8. Greater long-term strategy and investment – as speculative outside capital is locked out. Workers have a greater long-term interest in the firm and community.

9. Far less squandering of wealth created on speculative outside investors and ludicrously overpaid top management (like, remember the NASDAQ bubble?). Far less inherent conflict of interest within firm over forming capital – as workers own ALL of it. Potentially higher capital formation (realized in Mondragon federation and Washington state plywood firms), more efficiently used, feeds higher productivity and greater creativity. (Tax laws can distort this, individual capital accounts can enhance this.)

10. Socialization of entrepreneurial process/experience (ESPECIALLY as our firms federate) radically lowers an already low failure rate – which in turn lowers the risk premium our banks have to charge to cover bad debt and finance growth. Business failure also has a traumatic and demoralizing effect on those who go through it. Mondragon federation: 1% failure rate as a % of workers; French sector as a whole: 1.4% failure rate as a % of firms. The failure rate for U.S. capitalist franchises is 20%.

11. In time, as we understand and use our advantages, our sector will spread and attain VERTICAL INTEGRATION, linked with our own banking infrastructure, and permanently affordable (limited equity) home ownership for our workers. This will enable us to gain radical cost control. Free workers can exchange goods, services,

and property on terms of our own choosing – regardless of what is going on in the capitalist sector.

This will amplify the other structural advantages listed here and position us to permanently destroy capitalist hegemony.

FOR MORE INFORMATION IN THE U.S.A:

U.S. Federation of Worker Cooperatives
P.O. Box 170701
San Francisco, CA 94117

info@usworker.coop

FOOTNOTES

1. Survey by Cognetics, Inc., reported in Investors Business Daily, 11-6-96.

2. Standard & Poor data, reported in Wall St. Journal, 2-3-97.

3. Making Mondragon, Whyte & Whyte, 1986, p. 6 Industrial Democracy In Italy Mark Holstrom S.F. Chronicle 2-13-98

4. Labor-managed cooperatives and private firms in North Central Italy: an empirical comparison Will Bartlett, John Cable, Saul Estrin, Derek Jones, Stephen Smith c 1992 Cornell University

REFERENCES

When Workers Decide: Workplace Democracy Takes Root in North America c 1992 Len Krimmerman & Frank Lindenfeld New Society Publishers

Worker Cooperatives in America, Robert Jackall & Henry Levin c 1984 University of California Press

Making Mondragon William F. Whyte & Kathleen K. Whyte c 1988 Cornell University

The Democratic Worker-Owned Firm: a new model for East and West David Ellerman c 1990 Unwin Hyman, Inc.

The viability of employee-owned firms: evidence from France Saul Estrin & Derek Jones c 1992 Cornell University

We Own It Peter Honigsberg, Bernard Kamoroff, Jim Beatty c 1982 Bell Springs Publishing Liberation Management Tom Peters

Libertarian Labor Review Issue No. 19 (Winter 1996)

Update on a large example: (2012-13) Mondragon Cooperative Corporation

From The Guardian (UK) 6-24-12

- 85,000 worker-owners (2010 annual report).
- Enterprises average 80% - 85% worker-owners.
- Top paid executive members limited to earning 6.5 times the pay of the LOWEST PAID workers. (U.S. CEO's get 400 times the pay of the AVERAGE worker in their firm)
- 43% of MCC members are women.
- Rerearch and development (R&D) employs 800 members with a budget of $75 million. In 2010, 21.4% of total MCC sales were new products and services that did not exist 5 years earlier.
- MCC is Spain's 7th largest corporation.

- MCC's bank, Caja Laboral (Labor House) had $25 billion in deposits in 2010.
- Total student enrollment in all MCC educational centers was 9282 in 2010. MCC University had 3400 students in its 2009-10 year.

The Guardian (UK) 3-7-13

- MCC global sales 15 billion euros, total assets 35.9 billion euros.
- Employment grew from 25,479 in 1991 to 83,569 in 2011 (from MCC website).
- However, most of the 14,000 workers employed by MCC outside Spain are NOT owners.
- As of 2012, average pay has dropped 5% as a result of Spain's depression. Refrigerator and washing machine demand has collapsed by 50%; from this and cheap competition from Asia, Fagor, the MCC appliance maker (5600 workers) has been in serious trouble and was near bankruptcy as of Oct. 2013. As of the end of 2012, workers in shrinking firms have been employed in other member-firms, and there have been no layoffs. At this time Spanish unemployment was 26%.

Italy – entire country

54,200 worker-owned/self-managed enterprises, 963,300 member-owners, 312,843 non-members (many on track to become members) (2013, CICOPA – International Organization of Industrial, Artisanal, and Service Producers Co-operatives)

Meanwhile, in the capitalist sector . . .

Gallup does an annual survey of "employee engagement" in U.S. capitalist firms. In the latest (2013), only 30% of America's 100 million full-time employees were found to be "engaged" in their work. 50% were "not engaged", described as "sleep-walking through their jobs", and 20% were "actively disengaged" – i.e. actively undermining their employer's enterprise. This rises to 30% in firms that are "letting go" (firing/downsizing) workers, with the "engaged" falling to 13% in these firms. In all firms, only 41% of employees felt that they knew what "their" company stands for, and what makes its brand different than other brands.

So U.S. capitalist firms **already** have a large 5th column inside their enterprises – a stark testament to the inherent functional inferiority of capitalist work relations. And so the capitalist task-masters ask: "How can we increase employee engagement?" (**without** fundamentally changing the nature of work and who gets the wealth it creates.) This is like the rulers of China who ask: "How can we stop all this government corruption?" (**without** getting rid of the One-Party State that **inherently** creates it.) These are oxymoronic questions.

Most resistance of American workers to capitalism at this point is highly **individual**. Much like all the recent underwater home "owners" who simply stopped paying their bone-crushing mortgages while occupying the home as long as possible, aided by the shear volume of delinquencies. This is in fact a highly **individualist** mortgage strike. And it has proven to be far smarter than all the other home "owners" who kept paying while being deliberately strung along with promises of loan modification and immense mountains of deliberately mismanaged paperwork. They got foreclosed on **too**, got their credit-ratings trashed **too**, only after being had out of a **lot** more money. And by bankers who got a total of $700 billion in taxpayer-funded bailouts. Is ANYONE surprised? They're capitalists. How do you **expect** capitalists to behave?

As for our sector, the worker-owned/self-managed sector, there has been an ongoing news blackout on it in The Economist and the Wall St. Journal. Both publications avidly cover capitalist innovations, even when they are quite small. The Economist several years back even had very long special articles about the economies of Italy and Spain, with not a PEEP about their substantial worker-owned sectors. **Until something bad happened** that they could gloat about: the impending bankruptcy of Fagor, which employs about 6.5% of the Mondragon federation's workers (unemployment in Spain as a whole was 27% in 2013). **Both** publications had articles about **this**.

So we can be sure the class enemy is highly aware of us, small as we are at this point. This makes a collective capitalist strategy of economic strangulation virtually certain, as soon as we have grown to a sufficient perceived threat. And a perceived threat could simply be worker-ownership becoming known and popular, while our actually existing sector is still small and easier to strangle. This will force us to turn to our large (and growing, at this point) 5th column inside the capitalist sector. I despise Mao, but he said one thing I agree with: There are no rights, only power struggles.

Thought experiment:
Why capitalism can't be banned
(and shouldn't be even if it could)

This is called a thought experiment because it is about as likely to happen in America as a takeover by space aliens. But this Red Herring will be dragged across America by the Right, as the whole capitalist system slides deeper into a mass crisis of legitimacy. And it may even occur to opponents of capitalist rule: If capitalism is so toxic, creating all these horrible crises and diseases, shouldn't it be dealt with like DDT, Agent Orange, and smoking in enclosed public spaces?

The whole French-Russian model of revolution is so historically discredited that I have not addressed it extensively in this book. It worked fairly well in France, because self-management capacity is easier to quickly attain on a mass scale in an 18th century peasant economy. America now is a highly complex "post" industrial economy. I won't bother with the vast, genocidal disaster that was Stalin's Russia, which **no one** wants to repeat.

Even if banning capitalism was imposed on all of society directly by free working people, who had attained self-management capacity, you can't **force** people to be free. This is an oxymoron, though to a large extent, coming events will do this anyway. Necessity is the mother of invention. But even here, the inventors will be people who actually **want** to be free, can see to do it, and haven't invested their entire lives ideologically into capitalism. **Never** underestimate the power of a dearly held ideology to override all kinds of hard, pressing facts on the ground. Just look at all the Americans today who listen to **nothing** but Fox News and right-wing talk radio all day, and the deep capitalist crisis has just begun.

My first response here is: Those who worship the vast Whore of Babylon that is capitalism **deserve** to have it. **Provided that the rest of us don't have to have it too.**

This is easier said than done. As discussed in the Transitional Economics chapter of this book, worker-ownership/self-management will be subjected to economic strangulation by the still dominant capitalist sector as soon as it is a threat, real or perceived, to continued capitalist rule. This is certain, the only question is when. When could easily be at the point where worker-owned/self-managed enterprises account for as little as 5% of the U.S. economy.

Real, enduring fundamental systemic change has two basic aspects. One is organic displacement – the natural growth of worker-owned/self-managed enterprises and allied property forms like community development credit unions, permanently affordable housing cooperatives, and consumer cooperatives.

The other is rupture – where working people are **forced** to take power simply in order to defend our most basic rights. Economic strangulation of free workers can be countered with crippling mass upheaval inside the capitalist sector where most working people will still be. Violent repression, from either the private sector or the State, can be countered with self-defence and destruction of the enemy armed apparatus, which is why the 2nd Amendment is so critical. This will look more like the classic revolutionary model. But it will be **unable** to force freedom on working people who don't want it. **Any** attempt to do so will be a disaster, an enormous waste of effort badly needed elsewhere.

In a truly free society, everyone can have what they want, so long as it is not imposed on others. This is the genius of the libertarian/anarchist approach. There is **no** Politically Correct one-size-fits-all in a free society. The most seductive slogan that the economic Right came up with in the recent long period was Milton Freidman's Free to Choose. Our job is to make this a **reality**, not a formal pretense. The **real** agenda of the economic Right was well put by Margret Thatcher: There Is No Alternative. This goes very well with another infamous phrase of hers: There is no such thing as society. Late Capitalism has been very busy making this a reality.

There is another fundamental reason that a substantial capitalist sector must be free to exist for those who choose it. In a radically better future, working people who are born free, who have grown up and lived in freedom all their lives will have never tasted slavery. **Nothing** teaches you the value of freedom quicker than having it taken away. People who have never known bosses, landlords, exploitation/rent-gouging, bone-crushing mortgages, grinding commutes, and all the rest of that mess need to have this experience. This creates a strong immune system among those who are free. In a far brighter future, should the large capitalist rump ever become unable to compete and in danger of complete collapse, we would **subsidize** them. We'll **pay** them to do what they do, so no one **ever** forgets.

Unnatural Disasters

On the recent vast crown fire near Yosemite, David Bischel made some good points, concerning the clear-cutting of forest followed by fire suppression that made the whole mess to begin with (S.F. Chronicle, 8-30-13). Ignorant/stupid "land management" policies run by logging corporations and the (capitalist) State have resulted in vast, dense thickets of spindly, unhealthy trees, with small dead and dying branches running up them all. This is why we git these vast crown fires, which manage to destroy the healthy trees still left. Global warming means we will get a lot more of these fires.

But for a president of the California Forestry Association, Bischel displayed a shocking ignorance of how the Original People ("wild Indians") lived here. He writes as if no humans lived in northern/central California before the Europeans invaded. The "natural process" of low intensity fires he discusses that keep the forests healthy were in fact natural – deliberately set by the natural/wild humans who actually **knew** how to live here.

What the first European invaders (with all their plagues and guns) found here was an immense park. Huge, healthy, well-spaced trees, hundreds and even thousands of years old. Modest amounts (pure stands in chaparral) of trim, vigorous brush, free from massive amounts of dead and dying fire fuel. Plenty of native grasses and wildflowers, free from any masses of imported, invasive, noxious weeds like star thistle and broom.

Vast crown fires were completely unknown, and the far healthier forests and woodlands had greater biodiversity. This meant a lot more deer for the humans (and cougars and wolves), as well as a lot more acorn, manzanita berries, and nutritious greens for the humans (and bears and raccoons – tho neither knew how to pound and leech acorn). In small openings in the forest (deliberately cleared and maintained, which also improved forest health/ biodiversity and greatly raised acorn yield), as well as the open woodlands and grasslands, fields of brodeas ("Indian potatoes") were propagated by permaculture, to densities of 100 per square foot – radiant lavender in the Spring sun. See Tending the Wild, by M. Kat Anderson, and The Natural World of the California Indians, by Robert Heizer and Albert Elsasser for more on this.

Normal/wild humans do **not** voraciously overpopulate and relentlessly degrade the biosphere on which human life depends. Normal humans are an intimate, highly intelligent, inseparable part of this biosphere, and actually **improve** it, for all the other beings as well as themselves. Normal humans have an innately deep spiritual life, inseparable from all of daily life, and cannot even imagine a separate "thing" called "the environment" or "the wild". Or as Graham Harvey put it in Animism: Respect for the Living World – "The world is full of persons, only some of which are human."

All this will be hard for all the damaged, ignorant, enslaved humans we have here now to git. But it still lies latent in our damaged, but not destroyed, Deep Structure, which is nearly 2 million years old. This is a lot of why the movie Avatar had such wide appeal.

And guess what? The vast overpopulation of damaged humans we have now is **still** dependent on the biosphere. This biosphere does **not** depend on all these damaged humans. Jag Bhalla put it well: "Nature ultimately eliminates anything that damages what it depends on." (Scientific American, 7-12-13).

But there is very good news. The birth rate in much of the world, and nearly all the "developed" countries (which consume and pollute by far the most per capita), has fallen well **below** the replacement rate. Let's encourage/enable this to spread. (see Katha Pollit, in The Nation, 4-2-07, and S.F. Chronicle, 9-3-13). The alternative – massive chronic disease, genocidal war, plagues, and famines – will not be a happy one.

Rewilding sanctuary proposal

This would be for HUMANS, not just cougar-kitty and other persons who do not happen to be human. This would be an especially good home for raising kids, and we could also do rewilding retreats for comrades not fortunate enough to live on Land.

I have significant resources to plow into a human rewilding sanctuary, but not nearly enough to finance it myself. That will change if this book sells well.

The first task, obviously, is buying the Land (**somehow** "virtual Land" will not do. Don't **ask** me **why**!) This should be all-cash to be debt-free, and will also git the price down. Members would buy in at cost, with financing at CPI + 2% (a total of 3% interest at 2013 inflation rates). Interest portion above inflation would go into the project, not to me or any others putting up hard cash. Sweat equity would be proportional to market value added, to be determined by averaging 2 before and after appraisals. Every member would have an equity account, and we would want to git these up to rough equality as soon as possible. The ownership structure here would be similar to a limited-equity (permanently affordable) housing co-op. Sale (as opposed to buy-in) would only be at market value if the whole property was liquidated in order to move the sanctuary.

Northern California works well for me as I know the Land well. A big problem here is the marijuana industry and all the greed, paranoia, and crime/violence it attracts. One big reason I was forced to sell my original Land is that it is now surrounded closely on 3 sides by pot farms (legal/ medical marijuana as far as I know). At least they don't have to rape the Land to git their $$$. This problem will be reduced if pot is fully legalized, which in CA could easily happen by 2017.

Some notes on wild and permaculture food in Northern California

WARNING: Huntin' deer out of season without a deer tag can git you in big trouble. If you do this on yer own Land, yer own Land can even git confiscated by the State.

Salmon runs are hard to come by since all the dams got built, but there is other fishing. I don't think you can get in trouble for shooting wild turkeys and rabbits. Manzanita wood is very hard like mesquite, excellent for grilling and making jerky for storage. Wild game and fish are low in fat, live on organic/wild food, and are not factory-farmed under constant crowding/stress while fed hormones, constant antibiotics, and God knows what else. We can also raise our own chickens and rabbits, providing wild greens, leeched acorn, and garden/produce trimmings for food.

As you may already know, blueberries have the highest antioxidant content of any farmed produce. Wild whiteleaf manzanita berries (Arctostaphylos viscida) have 3 **times** the antioxidant concentration of farmed blueberries. This native bush is **extremely** common here at elevations of 1000 to 2500 ft.. The berries dry right on the plant for storage. Western lilac/deer brush (Ceanothus integerrimus) leaves are tender and mild tasting clear into July, and can be dried for storage. They contain catechins, a class of antioxidants also found in tea, and are a mild stimulant. This ceanothus is **extremely** common here at elevations of 2500 to 5000 ft.. Acorn has a nutritional profile similar to chestnuts; black oak and tan oak acorns were favored by the Original People as they have the highest protein and fat content. (Fat is not an issue for normal/wild humans, as they are physically active and do not suffer from eating disorders.) These two oak species are **extremely** common here – black oak between 1500 and 5000 ft., tan oak in the wetter climates between 2500 and 4500 ft. – lower near the coast. Pounding and leeching acorn takes far less time than waiting for olives to brine (you can't eat olives right off the tree either), and whole acorn stores for 2 years or more if dried.

A note on wild abundance: On the Land I know, you can't just eat off the Land any old time. Most wild food is only available at certain times and has to be dried or jerkied for storage. Some wild crops, like black oak acorn and whiteleaf manzantia berries, are hyperabundant – but only every other year. This is much like olives, and to some degree almonds, from the Mediterranean.

Patches of brodea can be regenerated by permaculture, as practiced by the Original People. They are not now abundant enough fully wild to dig up for food. Mediterranean crops – such as lentils, chickpeas, wheat, olives, pomegranites, grapes, Italian plums, hazelnuts, almonds – naturalize well in our Mediterranean climate, and can be grown by permaculture. Mediterranean herbs as well, which are highly nutritious and often medicinal (rosemary and sage are brain tonics, Mediterranean bay helps prevent cancer, oregano is potent with antioxidants). There are also very good wild herbs here, like yerba santa and western pennyroyal. Other produce and medicinal plants can be provided by organic gardening, and dried or root-cellared for when they are unavailable fresh. The Original People used our highly pungent native bay leaves to keep bugs out of stored food. Cleaning out dead brush, plus thinning brush and young trees where needed for the health of the forest, provides ultra-abundant wood for free heat in winter.

As for permaculture, granite, basalt, and limestone parent material makes good soil, metamorphic rock and sandstone very poor. The aiken clay loam (primarily granulated clay) on my original Land was very deep – the forest has been making it on basalt parent material for 3 million years. It has good structure – it is both permeable and holds water/nutrients well; the trees feed off of water banked in the very deep subsoil thru the hot summer dry season. Fertility is low, but that is easily added.

How many children of the invaders know **any** of this? God arrays abundance before us, we need to do little agricultural toil, but we are too blind to see it. (No! Food comes from the supermarket! Heat in winter comes from turning a dial! Shelter comes from landlords and real-estate speculators!)

In my case, I learned how to read topo maps from my Dad at age 6, and all the native trees, plants, and critters from A Natural History of the Sierra Nevada at age 7 and 8. Geology from my Dad, soil structure, climate, weather, and gardening on my own, at ages 8 to 10. All of this was a result of spontaneous interest, it was not imposed or even a result of deliberate instruction. The bond of normal/wild humans with the rest of nature spontaneously self-organizes given any opportunity (and I had quite a bit, for a non-normal/wild human). It is virtual instinct, arising from an enabled human Deep Structure nearly 2 million years old.

Other book proceeds:

Two obvious recipients will be the U.S. Federation of Worker Co-operatives and the Multidisciplinary Association for Psychedelic Studies. Also any Occupy-type political actions/projects that emerge.

The futility of art

Much has been made by the paleoanthropologists of our time about the lack of representational art in human societies before 40,000 years ago. These people are way too impressed by civilization, and lack the perspective of normal humans who are free from it. Lacking what has been called mystical experience, which was an everyday experience for fully normal humans, they do not understand why these humans did not bother with representational art.

I am not lacking in artistic ability, and my ability immediately improved very early in my work with psychedelics. But my best work was junk compared to what I could see with my own eyes in a full-blown mystical state. And I was not hallucinating – i.e. seeing anything that was not physically there (1). I was seeing what was right in front of me far more deeply, clearly, and subtly – making what we take to be eyesight blindness by comparison. I have also seen incredibly fine visions with my eyes shut.

I could not even begin to put any of this down on paper for others to see, even though my artwork greatly improved. My pitiful attempts to do so became so painful that I stopped (2). (I had wanted to do an exhibit titled "It's ALL LSD's fault!") I have not done any representational art in decades.

John Zerzan cites Jameson: ". . . art had no place in unfallen social reality because there was no need for it." Zerzan again: "Though art is not fundamentally concerned with beauty, its inability to rival nature sensuously has evoked many unfavorable comparisons." "All art, as symbolization, is rooted in the creation of substitutes, surrogates for something else; by its very nature therefore, it is falsification." (3)

More simply put, art is idolatry. The Emanation (Mother Earth and Father Sky), and the inmost, final Reality that this emanates from are One. Fully normal humans experienced this reality all the time, and so did not indulge in the pointless idolatry of art.

The paleoanthropologists of our time also make much out of fully normal human's lack of technological change. Fully normal/wild humans, who are deeply intimate with the rest of nature and very well adapted to it, deeply contented, and often in a state of unspeakable ecstasy, are not interested in this.

Agriculture, and all the mess that came after it, resulted from the loss of the Way. The endlessly accelerating frenzy of shallow, empty "innovation" we have now is in great part driven by deep, not fully conscious unhappiness, and only makes it worse. Computer software is rushed out the door 75% done, full of bugs, and is then hacked by increasingly skilled cybercriminals. The frenzy accelerates, making ever more $$$ for the techie capitalists.

This endlessly accelerating frenzy is the nihilists dream – destruction purely for its own sake. Its consummation, if fulfilled, will be the complete destruction of anything recognizably human.

I will touch briefly on another exercise in futility – philosophy. While the interdisciplinary reach of this book is fairly extensive, I have studied philosophy little and have even less interest in it. The nature of reality and the meaning of life is not a question the intellect is remotely capable of answering. The answer is far deeper, and can only be revealed directly/ experientially by God. Normal humans do not even ask this question because they already have been given the answer.

Much of the same could be said about theology. To a large degree, theology is to God what ideology is to problem-solving, only worse. You could spend years in a seminary and never know God, when a single day spent in the backwoods on 300 mcg. of LSD would do the job.

(1) Somehow, I have never managed to hallucinate on even 600 mcg. of LSD. Hallucinations are not what psychedelics are about, and I strongly object to psychedelics being referred to as "hallucinogens".

(2) At this time, someone said to me that I could create art that was better/more beautiful than nature itself. My immediate response, which I did not verbalize, was this: "My GOD! Are you BLIND?! How could you say something so radically ignorant?"

(3) John Zerzan, Elements of Refusal, pg. 62, 67, 66

God's Instrument:
DEMYSTIFYING "MYSTICISM"

WORKING WITH TRUE PSYCHEDELICS: LSD, psilocybin (in mushrooms), mescaline (in peyote), DMT (in ayahuasca). For those who don't know this, psychedelic is a Greek word. Psyche = mind, Delos = manifestation, Psychedelic = mind-manifesting.

Native Americans have had access to true psychedelics for thousands of years, understand why God gave them to us, and have used them with appropriate intent. Today in the U.S.A., the 250,000 members of the (highly decentralized) Native American Church work with psychedelics, primarily peyote. Courts and legislation have even ruled that this is legal. The Oklevueha Native American Church has some good material on their website (nativeamericanchurches.org), especially their Code of Ethics, which is excellent.

Imagine having been blind all your life and seeing for the first time ever. Imagine trying to describe this to other people who have also been blind all their lives. This Seeing was with my entire being, right down to its final core. This level of experience is accessible to all of us, and in fact was Intended for all of us.

The following was drawn from my own highly successful work with psychedelics. The success I was given is particularly striking because when I began this work, I was one of those "unstable personalities" that could be "most harmed" by LSD (to quote a 1966 Time magazine essay).

An important qualifier in my case, in addition to spiritual intent: I had held down a non-stressed filled, steady job for two and one-half years (for the first time in my life), had low rent (thanks to a socialist landlord), $7000 in the bank (in 2012 dollars), and had not suffered major depression for 2 straight years. I was 25. There was a hard, material foundation of security in my life, which greatly lessened the symptoms of my character disorder. An earlier tryout with psilocybin mushrooms, at age 22, when none of this was in place, and with unclear intent, did not go well.

1. Psychedelics should only be used with spiritual intent. This includes character revelation/reconstruction.
2. I was NEVER talked into taking psychedelics. The Call came from within, from what has been called the still, small voice.
3. I tried a small dose at first – 1 gram of psilocybin mushrooms, to be sure I was ready. I then worked with 2 grams around once or twice a month, and entered my first full-blown mystical state the second time I did this. Then LSD at 175 mcg., then 300 mcg., once or twice a month. When the LSD began bringing up difficult internal/ character material, I continued at 300 mcg., but less frequently – around once every 2 months. One time, when I needed to break down strongly held illusion/resistance, I went up to 600 mcg.. Several other times I went up to 400 mcg. The classic '60's dose was 250 mcg.. What I was getting was pharmaceutically pure or damn close to it – NO side effects at 600 mcg..
4. I NEVER mixed psychedelics with heavy drinking or drugs.

The following concern becoming capable of receiving mystical experience (Direct Knowledge). They can also apply to other, less high-impact methods than psychedelics.

5. Being taught directly by Reality (called "mystical experience" by this society) required the annihilation of my self-will/ego, intellectualization, and even thought. That inmost, final Reality which is selfless could only be approached in a selfless state. This annihilation made me teachable, and I could not handle a large dose of LSD. Reality/God handled it for me.

6. I could not possibly even begin to imagine the level of experience I was given in advance. What has been called mystical experience is far deeper than imagination. Preconception is even shallower/ less helpful than imagination. God annihilated both. This is why Direct Knowledge cannot be described or explained. To a limited level, it is possible to speak from it. It has been said about God and heaven: "How can you buy real estate, sight unseen?" I have seen the real estate.

7. I almost always worked with psychedelics in the backwoods. God's temple has already been built – it is called Mother Earth and Father Sky. God did not cast us out of Eden, WE CAST OURSELVES OUT. And Eden remains, waiting for our Return.

8. I was first, for an entire year, shown what was possible in my life. This could be called unspeakable ecstasy/gratitude, transcending pleasure and pain, and this does not even begin to do it justice. To paraphrase Eben Alexander: We, and the entire known universe, emanate from an inmost, final Reality that " loves us more deeply and fiercely than any human ever loved their own child". But it is idolatry to even attempt description of what has been called the mystical state. Then the difficult stuff: what in my character was in the way. This can be very hard. Many of the original hippies turned to heavy drinking and narcotics when the LSD sessions turned difficult.

9. If you have a cruel, demanding parent in your head (primitive, sadistic superego in Doctor Talk) it is very easy to confuse this with God, even after being taught directly by God. This makes the revelation of character pathology, and character reconstruction a LOT more difficult.

10. Looking deeper than the term character defects used by 12-step, it was more helpful to see the entire character structure as a whole. Then I could see what the character defects came from, what motivated them, and how they formed. There are 3 broad developmental stages in the original, childhood formation

of character structure: Attachment formation (1st year of life), Individuation (ages 1-3), gender formation/Oedipal stage (ages 3-6). These are critical effect periods, essential to the enablement of the entire human Deep Structure. I was lead to the appropriate psychiatric texts.

The Multidisciplinary Association for Psychedelic Studies (MAPS) (maps.org) is an excellent resource. They have a very good paper on their website on working with difficult psychedelic experiences. Not all my experiences with psychedelics were ecstatic. The hardest, messiest work I have ever done in my life was on large doses of LSD. But I never feared. God was palpably with me the entire time. I never had a psychiatric emergency, or even anything I would label a "bad trip".

Nearly 50 years after the Summer of Love, all the ensuing hysteria has finally died down enough that legal, FDA-approved research has begun on psychedelics. (All my work with psychedelics would be FELONIES!) Psychedelics show great promise with work on post-traumatic stress disorder, drug and alcohol addiction, and end of life issues.

GENERAL DISCLAIMER

The content presented in this chapter (and book) is for informational purposes only, and should not be construed as a substitute for medical or mental health care. John Burnett expressly does not provide any medical, psychological, diagnostic, counseling or treatment services. John Burnett shall not be liable for claims or damages, and expressly disclaims any and all liability of any nature for any action, or non-action, taken as a result of the information presented in this book. Use of this book is at the sole discretion and responsibility of the individual reader.

HAZARD COMPARISON: LSD and NARCOTICS

	USERS (2012)	HOSPITAL VISITS (2011) %	
LSD	1.1 million	5000	0.45%

NARCOTICS

Cocaine + crack	4.72 million	505,000	10.7%
Oxycodone	1.5 million	151,000	10.1%
Meth	1.2 million	103,000	8.6%
Heroin	669,000	258,000	38.6%

(Source: Time, 9-8-14 from SAMHSA data)

ADDICTIVENESS

LSD: 0

NARCOTICS:Cocaine – 50,Crack – 100,Oxycodone – 40,Meth – 75,Heroin – 80

(Scale of 0 to 100. Source: Time, 9-8-14, citing Lawrence Phillips, London School of Economics, and David Nutt, Imperial College of London, based on the opinion of addiction experts.)

COMMENTARY

You have to wonder here, what all the 1960's hysteria was about. A big factor is that the average "hit" of LSD now is almost certainly a lower dose than the classic '60's dose of 250 mcg. In the 1980's, when I was working with LSD, the dosage I was getting was 100 mcg. or 175 mcg. per "hit". I titrated it much higher by conscious, informed choice. I would not recommend doing your first ever LSD session on 250 mcg.

Also, in my case, difficult LSD sessions had no shock value. I already had years of chronic major depression under my belt. This time, with LSD, the heavy pain was not meaningless but radically constructive. I understood what I was getting into and what I had to do. And if I did it, the pain would in time lift, and the possibilities I had been shown many times would start to happen. They did. Since 1987, I have had major depression briefly once, when I was planning to commit a serious act of capitalism and from this ruptured my relationship with God. I have no need to be on antidepressants, despite many years of major depression in my youth, which makes most people chronically vulnerable to major depression for life.

Finally, the whole point of conscious work with LSD is to reach the level where your will is in such alignment with the intent of Reality that you can receive a full-blown mystical state (Direct Knowledge) without any LSD at all. I'm not there yet, but this did happen once. It occurred after a period of deep spiritual study and contemplation, and immediately resulted in a permanent, radical change in my character structure. I was up in a tree doing a pruning job when it started. (No, I did not fall out of the tree.)

Even with psychedelics, I did not fully "come down" after receiving Direct Knowledge, far less forget the experience. And the experience did not need to be integrated. It integrated itself. There is a deep, long afterglow of immense gratitude that does not lead to craving.

As it is now in my life, borderline mystical states are common.(1)My most recent session with psychedelics (psilocybin) was in 1997.

(1) When I remember experience that was given to me as long as 31 years ago, I choke up, sometimes to the point of crying, in a state of shear gratitude. This can be triggered by certain music, or certain words in my mind, or by intimacy with wild Land. This may be what is called Dhikr – remembrance (of God) in Islamic mysticism. Part of what is happening here is that I'm beginning to open up to this level of experience in the present.

Some helpful quotations

"Scripture is an attempt to translate what cannot be translated." -author, 1989

"Zen may lose all its literature, all its monasteries, and all its paraphernalia; but as long as there is satori in it it will survive to eternity. …the opening of satori is the remaking of life itself." (D.T. Suzuki, Essays in Zen Buddhism, 1st series, pg. 230-231)

"Everyone who comes to me and listens to my words and acts on them – I will show you what he is like. He is like the man who when he built his house dug deep, and laid the foundations on rock; when the river was in flood it bore down on that house but could not shake it, it was so well built."(Luke 6: 47-48)

"…the peace or poverty (for peace is only possible in poverty) is only obtained after a fierce battle fought with the entire strength of your personality. Without it, whatever peace that obtains is a simulacrum, and has no deep foundation; the first storm it may encounter will crush it to the ground. Zen is quite emphatic in this.(D.T. Suzuki, ibid, pg. 27)

"Far from relying on any power of my own, I came among you in great fear and trembling; and in my speech there was none of the arguments that belong to philosophy, only a demonstration of the power of the Spirit."(Corinthians 2: 4)

"We teach what scripture calls: *the things no eye has seen and no ear has heard, things beyond the mind of man, all that God has prepared for those who love God."* (Corinthians 2: 9)

"I shall destroy the wisdom of the wise and bring to nothing all the learning of the learned."(Corinthians 1: 9)

"There are no births, no signs, no clinging, no abandoning; in the mind of the bodhisattva there is no going-out, no coming-in. When this mind which neither goes out nor comes in enters into that which is never entered into, it is called entering. This is the way that the bodhisattva enters into the Dharma... It is neither mind nor shadows, it is pure in its suchness. (Vajrasamadhi-sutra, quoted by D.T. Suzuki, ibid, pg. 184)

Author's note: Satori and Samadhi roughly "translate" as the full-blown mystical state or Direct Knowledge. Dharma roughly translates as the Way or Tao.

Individual character structure and its fundamental reconstruction
(some notes from my internal work, 1984-1989)

"OTTO KERNBERG ON LSD"* (1985)

Levels of character organization, from most to least evolved:

ENLIGHTENMENT

Totally unselfish – no ego or self as we understand it; totally able to let go of and love others. Total insight, one with what Is. Direct access to higher parallel universes, which advanced physics has already posited.

"I am awake." - the Buddha

MATURITY

Clearer levels of true empathy (as opposed to projection) and unselfish behavior; greater capacity to let go of and love others; clearer and deeper insight into self and others, with progressive removal of one's ego altogether.

NEUROSES

"Normal" people (though most narcissists function and appear "normal" in this society). Functionally coherent and integrated ego; functional ability to distinguish one's own ego from other's; functional give-and-take in relationships, though often selfish. Unconscious to preconscious sexual/gender conflicts, with anal conflicts in obsessive-compulsive personalities.

BORDERLINE CONDITIONS

Narcissistic and borderline personalities most common of these. Manipulative, parasitic, often clinging relationships with others as partially separated extensions of one's own ego, which is weak and fragmented (note:

superficially cohesive in narcissists). "Fuzzy" boundaries; very self-involved, often with grandiose fantasies (actual self-image in narcissists). Condensed sexual/gender and pre-gender/sexual conflicts. Often impaired but reasonably intact ability to get by in this society.

PSYCHOSES "Create your own reality!"

Greater ego diffusion with loss of ability to distinguish reality from distortion and full-blown delusion; little ability to connect with others, severely impaired to nearly non-existent functioning.

THE BOTTOMLESS PIT

No ego boundaries, totally unable to let go of and love others; little or no real insight and no real interest in it (there is often an elaborate and convoluted pretense to the contrary); totally selfish, total ego diffusion, to the point of aiming to possess the souls of others (soul murder). Paradoxically, a very advanced capacity for manipulation; surface level functioning is very often good to excellent. What has been called the demonic or Satanic realm is a parallel universe that intersects with our known universe. It is like a severely hierarchical series of holding companies – every being in it is Possessed. It is the Final Capitalism.

(THE ABOVE WAS TRANSCRIBED FROM A FULL-COLOR PSYCHEDELIC POSTER I DID LATE 1985, with some recent elaboration.)

"OTTO KERNBERG ON LSD"
Some additional notes (1988)

"Oneness" or "Enlightenment" to the narcissistically deluded is an (unconscious) backward regression towards ego diffusion, rather than a forward maturation towards ego transcendence. It is a grandiose escape from the difficult and "mundane" work of attaining mental health. Instead, the sick ego regresses further and can finally attempt to swallow external reality.

Some basic structural characteristics of highly evolved individuals:

1. Lucid perception and deep empathy result in great part from fantastically clear self/other differentiation. Perception is as wide open as if one was on a large dose of LSD, and at the same time there is no projection of internal material into one's perception of others. Paradoxically, absolute otherness is the basis of true oneness.

2. There is complete self-knowledge. All unconscious material has been made conscious and can be completely accessed at will. In a real sense, there is no unconscious at all.

3. Many basic structural characteristics of mental health can be seen as primitive forerunners of highly evolved states: Object constancy and the end of splitting are forerunners of the end of dualism. Sublimation is a forerunner of ego-transcendence. Aggression is completely bonded with libido; all instinctual drives have been absorbed into the higher chakras and radically altered. Individuation, which is spontaneous and can only emerge from within, is a forerunner of Self Realization.

The healthy ego of one who is individuated is finally a delusion, but it is qualitatively and radically closer to Reality than the pathological ego of one who has a narcissistic disorder (and clinical false self). (Note – in a nutshell, Kernberg defines individuation as the full flowering of the ability for creativity and intimacy.)

You must find yourself inorder to lose yourself.

(*) No, Otto Kernberg did NOT write this chapter while on LSD (I suspect he would be APPALLED at the suggestion). This is my work.

Some resources

LSD and psilocybin (I would include a page of high-quality "blotter acid", but THAT would be "drug trafficking".)

The Four Gospels

The Bhagavad Gita (The Song of God)

A General Theory of Love,   Lewis, Amini, and Lannon, 2000

Attachment,   John Bolby 1969, 1982

The Culture of Narcissism,   Christopher Lasch, 1979

The Borderline and Narcissistic Disorders,   James Masterson, 1975

People of the Lie,   Scott Peck, 1983

Borderline Conditions and Pathological Narcissism,
Otto Kernberg, 1975

Aggression in Severe Personality Disorders,   Otto Kernberg, 1995

Love Relations,   Otto Kernberg, 1998

Love relations during the Emancipation

I was somewhat surprised to read in Time (12-2-13) that teenage boys still fall in love. (Not having teenage boys of my own, I wouldn't know.) Apparently the techie-sex-saturated hookup-culture we have now has not completely destroyed this basic part of the normal human Deep Structure.

A central aim of the Emancipation will be the regeneration of the normal human primacy of affection and love over sex. Neurobiologically (for men), oxytocin over testosterone – a strengthening oxytocin system will absorb and dominate the testosterone system.

Among other things, this will not only eliminate promiscuity, hyperpromiscuity, and serial infatuation (from lack of interest), it will also defuse sexual possessiveness and intrigue. This will enable the regeneration of the co-operative/collective human relationships that are the necessary precondition for the normal upbringing of human young. Even more immediately, it will enable the resilience needed to cope with all the socioeconomic crisis and disease that Late Capitalism is gracing our lives with (with much more to come).

Since the Fall, a spiritual practice emerged in Hinduism and Buddhism called Tantra, which is directly related to the above. It involves removing the blockage obstructing the normal flow of sexual energy/desire into what are called the higher Chakras – particularly the 4th Chakra (called the heart in the West) and the 6th Chakra (also called the 3rd eye, which concerns spiritual discernment).

In the West, the approach to damaged sexuality has been to just stifle and persecute it, which is far less helpful (a vast understatement). The postmodern revolt against this in the West has involved little more than giving this damaged sexuality free reign, which has resulted in a whole new set of problems, some of them, like the HIV/AIDS plague, even worse.

The biggest counterforce to all this galloping sexual degeneracy is the growing emancipation of women. This draws from the human Deep Structure, and the species-memory of the nearly 2 million years that normal humans had gender equality. It is fairly obvious that the completion and consolidation of this emancipation will require women's primary emotional commitment be to each other. As in Sisterhood is Powerful. If women are preoccupied with nasty gossip and fights over men (particularly if the men in question are pigs), the emancipation of women is not coming anytime soon. Women's choice of what man they are intimate with will extend to the choice of whether to be intimate with a man at all. A good choice to be able to have, given how damaged we all are.

The recent erosion of homophobia is surprising to me. I remember how bad it was in the 1970's and 1980's. This too draws from the human Deep Structure. I discussed earlier how male love (not necessarily sexualized) was central to the very formation of humans. The word tight buddy has been around a long time, but two new words have recently emerged in (straight) male culture, particularly among those under 35: guy-crush and bro-mance. Unlike tight buddy, these baldly imply an erotic element, even if this is not acted out. I never thought I'd see this in my lifetime.

Feminism and the emancipation of male love will hugely help with the regeneration of the normal male and female collectives necessary for the normal upbringing of human young. Even in a vast sea of Late Capitalist degeneracy, the normal human Deep Structure is waking up.

A little on my own history. When I was a kid, there were 4 grade school buddies who loved me, and who I was in love with, though I did not understand it in these terms at all. It never occurred to any of us to do sex-play with each other (I didn't even know homosexuality existed), and none of these guys turned out gay (one of my several Brokeback Mountain tragedies). I was also tight with my dad until age 12. My sexuality (unconsciously) developed fused to my higher Chakras, sublimated, and collective in nature.

What a bad scene to discover in high school (1971-1975) that I was gay, when there was already a LOT of trouble going on at home. And then after this, having nowhere else to go with it but the gay subculture. To avoid a long digression on the (Late Capitalist) gay male subculture, I will cite one recent (2006) large study: over 2000 respondents on 96 questions, with the addition of hundreds of in depth, face-to-face interviews (Dynamic Duos, Keith Swain, 2008). Only 13% were in relationships, and THIS at a time when it was much easier to be gay than in the 1970's or 1980's. All the media attention on gay marriage is misleading, at least in the case of gay men. (NEVER MIND whether this heterosexual construct is appropriate to impose on male love. Like, how are 3 tight buddies supposed to "git married"? Guys join blood, as it was from the very formation of humankind.)

A final note here. The primacy of affection and love over sex is the door to a level of experience unimaginably deeper and finer than any sexual love. It is a subset of what has been called "mystical experience".

What I have called Tantra is an innate spiritual capacity in all humans. I have high aptitude for it because I had the very good formative experience of being in love with my tight buddies as a kid. Tantra is what Jonathan and David did (1st Book of Samuel, referred to at the beginning of the 2nd) even though there was no Tantra Yoga in ancient Israel. This is why there is no Biblical account of John and Dave ever having sex, even though they were flagrantly in love with each other. John and Dave did not shoot cum with each other. They saw God with each other.

". . . and they kissed one another, and wept with one another, until David exceeded." (1 Samuel 20:41)

"I am distressed for you, my brother Jonathan; very pleasant have you been unto me; your love to me was wonderful, passing the love of women." (2 Samuel 1:26)

Dave's buddy died in combat. They were war buddies. It was Dave who killed Goliath.

None of this implies that male love is inherently superior to heterosexual love. The heterosexual love of David's time was patriarchally deformed (as is the Bible), and though Dave was passionately in love with several women, he was never Tantric with a woman.

You have heard it said: till death do us part. Understand that love at this level does not suffer the destruction of the body. It is finally as birthless and deathless as the inmost Reality that it directly emanates from.

When the Return is fulfilled, love at this level will become normal among humans.

"If there is a good, all-powerful God, then why does He allow . . ."

For starters, God is not a "He".

"Horrible big earthquakes, that maim and kill many" A minor nuisance for normal humans living in villages of tule huts or simple cedar-plank houses. God never intended us to "live" in gigantic crowded cities.

"Plagues and famines" These do not exist in normal human societies. This started with agriculture and the first class societies, and got worse with crowded cities full of poverty resulting from exploitation. God never intended any of this for us.

"Giant tsunamis that maim and kill many" Normal humans sense them coming (the signs are obvious to those deeply intimate with the rest of nature), simply pick up their necessities, and move inland. Another nuisance. God never intended us to live in crowded cities on the coast.

"Protracted death-agony from all these incurable cancers" These are very rare in normal human societies. Widespread cancer is caused by unhealthy, unfree, stress-filled, polluted, and increasingly meaningless lives, which God **never** intended for us. What protracted death-agony did exist in normal human societies was quickly ended with euthanasia. Normal humans are not hung-up about death, and people who have seen God do not fear death.

"All the chronic suffering from diabetes, and strokes/heart attacks from hypertension" These do not exist in normal human societies.

"All the chronic suffering from major depression and other chronic mental illnesses" These do not exist in normal human societies.

"All the suffering from the exploitation, abuse, and lack of freedom that goes on" These conditions are not allowed to exist in normal human societies.

"All these horrible, vast forest fires that go on in the American West" These did not exist when normal humans lived here – see the chapter Unnatural Disasters.

God does NOT create or allow to go on all this suffering. WE CREATE IT because we do not live the way God intended us to live. This Way will be shown **directly** to any of us who open ourselves deeply enough.

NOTE: I am **hardly** advocating dumping the entire vast overpopulation of the L.A. basin into the Central Valley and the backwoods, then expecting everyone to **suddenly** become normal humans. (**Never mind** carrying capacity.) This is the "critique" of a straw man. The transition will take generations, and the first pioneers of the Return will be few.

This transition will require a massive conversion to green technology, massively less "resource" consumption/biosphere degradation, and massively less waste (1). This transition will also require doing everything to encourage/enable a birth rate well below the replacement rate for generations. A spreading capacity to receive what has been called mystical experience (Direct Knowledge) will mean more people will **want** to begin the Return, and in fact insist on it.

The alternative to this process will be exceedingly ugly, and blaming God for the results of our own willful ignorance will not help any.

(1) A very good place to start here is **ending** the twice-a-day, slow-motion mass cattle run known as commuting. **Nobody** wants this shit - it is forced on people who have to work for a living by a stupid, evil system. Ending this will require the reorganization of work, the expansion of mass transit, and making affordable housing available near work – by any means necessary.

The path of Jesus is communist

Do not lay up for yourselves treasures on Earth, where moth eat and rust consume, and where thieves break in and steal. For where your treasure is, there will be your heart also.

The eye is the lamp of the body. So if your eye is clear, your whole body will be full of light; but if your eye is soiled, your whole body will be full of darkness. If then the light in you is darkness, how great is the darkness.

No one can serve two masters; for either he will hate the one and love the other, or he will be devoted to the one and despise the other. You cannot serve God and mammon. (Matthew 6:19-24)

And when they prayed, the place in which they were gathered together was shaken; and they were all filled with the Holy Spirit and spoke the work of God with boldness. Now the company of those who believed were of one heart and soul, and no one said that any of the things which he possessed was his own, but they had everything in common. And with great power the apostles gave their testimony to the resurrection of the Lord Jesus, and great grace was upon them all. There was not a needy person among them, for as many as were possessors of lands or houses sold them, and brought the proceeds of what was sold and laid it at the apostle's feet; and distribution was made to each as they had need. (Acts 4:31-35)

MARK

9:35 Whoever wishes to be first must be last of all and servant of all.

10:17-27 It is easier for a camel to pass through a needle than for a rich man to enter the Kingdom of God.

10:42-45 similar to 9:35

11:15-19 moneychangers driven out of the temple

MATTHEW

6:19-24 God and mammon

6:25-34 lilies of the field

19:16-26 similar to Mark 10:17-27

21:12-16 similar to Mark 11:15-19

23:1-12 Do not let yourselves be called Rabbi; for you have one teacher, but you are all brothers

25:31-46 I was hungry and you fed me

LUKE

1:46-55 He has pulled down the dynasts from their thrones and raised up the humble

6:20-26 from the Beattitudes

6:39-40 Nor is the disciple above the teacher, but every disciple will end by being like his teacher

12:13-34 on hoarding possessions

14:33 Any of you who does not renounce all his possessions cannot be my disciple.

16:14-15 What is exalted among men is an abomination in the sight of God.

16:19-31 the rich man and Lazarus

18:18-27 similar to Mark 10:17-27

19:1-10 See, Lord, I am giving half of my possessions to the poor, and if I have made anything dishonestly at someone's expense, I give it back fourfold.

JOHN

2:13-17 similar to Mark 11:15-19

6:1-15 miracle of the loaves and fishes; Jesus withdraws from being made king

ACTS

    2:42-47 communism

    4:32-37 communism

    5:1-11 the fraud of Ananias and Sapphira

    6:1-6 elections to manage distribution of food

    10:1-35 God favors no nation

FIRST CORINTHIANS

    1:18-31 Those whom the world thinks common and contemptible are the ones God has chosen – those who are nothing at all to show up those who are everything.

REVELATION

    18:1-24 The destruction of Babylon

(At top: Matthew from Richmond Lattimore's translation from the Greek, Acts from Revised Standard edition of the Bible.)

Temptation (and envy)

Temptation is a preoccupation of Christians. What is poorly understood here is that all temptation to what Christians call sin is a result of delusion or spiritual blindness. (In more scientific terms, it is the result of a damaged human Deep Structure.) A selfish act that is harmful to others, or the Land (and ultimately oneself) is tempting if we feel there is something to be had from that act that is desirable. One who has Seen knows that there is nothing there worth having. This is not an intellectual process or an act of dutiful restraint. The true nature of the delusion is seen through with your entire being. And there is already a large body of experience with what **is** worth having.

It is a standard line of capitalist ideologues that people who don't like capitalism (the addiction to capital) are simply motivated by envy of the rich. There is often a large amount of truth to this claim.(1) It is also highly self-serving. Consumed with greed, capitalist ideologues need to believe everyone else is really like them. And this ignores the fact that working people, including those who exist in the vast, hot, shit-filled slums of Dubai and Mumbai (and well over 1 billion people worldwide are condemned to these capitalist Gulags), are paying for the vast wealth of these depraved individuals.

An article in the U.K. guardian (one of those cited in the Transitional Economics chapter), noted that one of the 6 founders of the Mondragon federation lives in an ordinary flat and drives a Ford Fiesta. Imagine how wealthy he would be if he was a founder of a capitalist firm employing 85,000 mostly skilled workers! The simple life of Pope Francis, who could easily live lavishly, has gotten media attention. What is poorly understood here is that this is not dutiful renunciation. These individuals are simply not interested in being wealthy.

What also has to be understood is that worker-owned/self-managed enterprises, built out of nothing but the effort of free working people, will not even be allowed to exist as soon as they become a serious ideological threat to the wealthy, should this oligarchy get its way. These questions finally won't be settled in the world of ideas – but by real power on the ground (refer to the chapters Transitional Economics and What It Will Take to Win).

(1.) The rather squalid lifestyle of Michael Moore, the famed Leftist filmmaker (from a working-class background), recently came to light in a divorce settlement, and was cause for much gloating among the worshippers of capitalism. Moore's $30 million net worth, with 9 houses and a 10,000 sq. ft. lakeside mansion in the North of Michigan, is of course peanuts compared to the $150 billion fortune of the Koch brothers. Ah, no matter how much you have, there is always someone else with vastly more. It never ends!

(Deliver in a Truman Capote voice)

Ameliorate America
NATIONAL COALITION FOR THE AMELIORATION OF ECONOMIC SLAVERY

We will rouse America with this inspiring slogan:

"An economy that works a little bit better for everyone."

To show how non-threatening we are, we will only allow bazzillionares like Warren Buffet to speak for us.

To show how SERIOUS we are, we will work TIRELESSLY for every Democratic Party politician.

To show that we understand the importance of mass action, we will hold a National Whine-In for a Better World once a year (see attached flyer).

To implement our inspiring slogan, we make the following BOLD requests:

1. A $499 annual renters credit in high-rent areas.
2. A $499 credit for 1st time homebuyers, plus a 4.99% reduction in the principle owed by home "owners" who are at least 20% underwater.
3. A $499 annual stipend to purchase health insurance from insurance companies.
4. A $499 annual stipend to attend college full-time.

5. A $199 annual stipend for commuters to purchase gas in congested urban areas.

To be paid for with a 1% increase in the tax rate on capital gains, dividends, and interest, plus a 1% annual tax on short-term financial transactions.

America, Rise and Whine!

Whine and Dine at the
30th Annual

WHINE-IN

FOR A BETTER WORLD

"Let's snivel our way to emancipation!"

- Wander aimlessly in a prescribed area.
- Chant prescribed slogans.
- Hear the same "militantly" whiny speeches that have been given for a generation.
- DO NOTHING!
- Wonder WHY things don't get better.

CONCRETE PROPOSALS shall be limited to whining "militantly" for hand-outs from the (capitalist) State. Paid for (inexorably) by higher taxes on the working class. We can't imagine WHY . . .

COMING EVENTS:

TEACH-IN   Leading experts on the awfulness of capitalism will teach you how to Whine Correctly!

GENERAL WHINE   We all show up at work as usual, but at a given hour, we all WHINE SIMULTANEOUSLY! Remember – don't DO anything, just whine.

FORBIDDEN SUBJECTS: 1. Irregular strikes /actions, sit-down strikes, and general strikes. 2. Mass rent and mortgage strikes. 3. Mass shutdowns of Wall St., K St., and other nerve centers of the global capitalist oligarchy. 4. Creation and growth of worker-owned/self-managed enterprises, permanently affordable housing co-ops, community development credit unions, and other economic organizations of a free working class. 5. Defense of the 2nd Amendment. "It's NOT about duck hunting." 6. Direct self-emancipation and self-defense for women, oppressed nationalities, and gay people.

Trivial Riot
Commentary on Bay Area News Group's coverage of the July 8, 2010 Oscar Grant event

I strongly agreed with the B.A.N.G. (Oakland Tribune, West County Times, San Jose Mercury) version of the Oscar Grant events, until I got other eyewitness sources.

Among the Oakland residents arrested were Oakland School Board member Jurnoke Hinton Hodge, a 69 year old former school principal, journalists, and legal observers, including Oakland attorney Walter Riley. Riley had this to say: "The police helped perpetuate a narrative of violence by allowing a small number of people vandalize businesses when they could have stopped it." Police arrested many demonstrators who did no violence, and then held them for days. They even beat old people, according to eyewitnesses. The National Lawyers Guild is preparing a lawsuit. The Bay Area News Group blacked all this out.

I don't doubt that B.A.N.G.'s account of the 200 rioters is largely or entirely true. The problem is that B.A.N.G. lied by omission. But alas! There is a split in the Capitalist press. The S.F. Chronicle covered a lot of this information. How is B.A.N.G. going to account for its news blackout/self-censorship?

The relative handful of trivial, puerile nihilists that rioted, given that they came from outside and for the most part chose really inappropriate targets (i.e. mom-and-pop coffee shops and lunch stops), are pseudo-radical tools of a Capitalist agenda. And I don't doubt for a minute that they were egged on by agent provocateurs. What a wonderful opportunity to make real radicals look bad in the community. They even looted a beauty shop, according to a friend of 35 years who has lived in Oakland for 30 years. Like, how trivial can you get? This inspired in me a bold new transitional demand: Why stop with wrinkle cream and hair color? Get serious: free cosmetic surgery ON DEMAND! Glamour for The People! SURELY this aroused aspiration among the Toiling Masses will bring the Capitalist System to its knees!

There is a much bigger, uglier parallel. During the protests at the World Trade Organization meeting in Genoa, Italy, in August of 2001 (up to 500,000 protesters showed up), police agents dressed up as Black Blockers (a small anarchist faction that fetishizes violence) invaded working-class neighborhoods and destroyed people's cars. At the same time, police invaded the headquarters of the protest coalition and beat dozens of people really bad, some to the point of near death. LOTS of trips to the ER. It should be noted that Italy's still sizable Fascist party has a large presence inside their police. I am reminded of a Newsweek account of the Iranian "Revolutionary Guard" crushing a vast protest against the recent fraudulent elections there. Ambulances were waiting. The hired thugs had instructions: crush the protesters, but don't kill them like the Shah did.

The Italian events were a national scandal until overshadowed by the 9-11 spectacle.

All of this is called Psyopts (psychological operations).

Differences among those who want change

Very broadly defined, the U.S. economic Left peaked at 66% of adults in late Oct. 2011, during the Occupy protests. This is the number who told the New York Times/CBS poll that wealth and income in the U.S. should be more equally distributed. 26% said it is fair the way it is now (10-24-11). By Feb. 2014, those wanting more equality had shrunk a little to 63%, with those saying it is fair now rising to 31%. In Jan. 2014, 60% told Pew Research that the economic system unfairly favors the wealthy, 36% disagreed (1-23-14). In addition, 40% respond negatively to the word "capitalism" (Pew, 2011), and 47% identify as "working class" as opposed to "middle class" (NORC, 2010). (1)

Actually existing capitalism in the U.S. is already discredited enough that even economic right-wing pundits are starting to frame their arguments in terms of "reducing inequality" and "creating opportunity" for working people. Some have even endorsed raising the minimum wage, and many endorse strengthening/expanding the Earned Income Tax Credit.

There will not be a consensus among those who want change of some kind. The Ameliorate America set will continue to do their thing, regardless of how much they are hectored by those who want fundamental change. For Ameliorate America's leaders, political careers, big campaign contributions, and plush consulting jobs are at stake. The Trivial Riot set will continue to loot beauty shops when the opportunity arises, regardless of how many times I or other radicals denounce them.

Those who want fundamental change are not yet clear about what to do (which is a big reason why few are **doing** anything right now), and will come to different conclusions. Our number is **far** larger than the number who self-identify as radical (see the chapter What's In a Word?). Most of us will be practical: what is actually starting to work? There is no common strategy that can be imposed on everyone, and any attempts to do so will aggravate rather than resolve differences.

The 40% of Americans who don't like capitalism is a **lot** of people (50% respond positively to the word). For the wealthy oligarchy, this is already the beginning of a mass crisis of legitimacy. Even larger numbers will shed their illusions, as conditions get inexorably worse, with occasional pauses. Denial, adaption, and escapism will become increasingly poor options.

The important thing is to study what works, even on a small scale, and then begin to **act**. People have different abilities and interests, and there is no need for all of us to agree on everything. Study what works, **do** something, and study the results. Learn from what others are doing, even if it is very different. When large numbers act, huge new opportunities open up, and what works will change and greatly expand.

I have discussed electoral activity very little in this book, though I don't entirely dismiss it (bad, BAD anarchist!). Nobody needs to get a president elected, or win a state ballot initiative, in order to conduct an irregular strike or action at work, a rent/mortgage strike, start a worker-owned/self-managed enterprise, or a self-help group. These are all highly effective actions. Self-management in particular is a highly effective capacity, and the critical mass for it to work can be shockingly small. And it tends to grow.

"'The 1% in America right now is still a bit lower than the 1% in pre-revolutionary France but is getting closer' says Piketty. . . . the stark historical consequences of unchecked inequality are at the heart of Capital." (Time magazine on Thomas Piketty's book, Capital in the 21st Century, 5-19-14)

The wealthy and near-wealthy know they are relentlessly destabilizing their own system, but they can't stop. Their disease, and the inherently diseased nature of their system, will continue to relentlessly grind down the rest of us. At what point will people finally snap and rise up? Many tens of millions of Americans already have little or nothing to lose, and their number will only grow. One of our national anthems calls America "land of the free and home of the brave". Both have been sorely missing here for a long time. At some point we have to decide whether or not America is a culture in terminal decline. What might cause serious numbers of Americans to finally find their bravery? Humiliation. There is already plenty of this around, but at some point the capitalist oligarchy (and their yuppie minions) will do something that is finally the last straw. This is almost inevitable.

At this point, the Ameliorate America set will find themselves starkly out of touch with where huge and rapidly growing numbers of Americans are at. The question at this point will be this: Do those of us who want fundamental change know what it will take to win?

(1) These last two are more significant to fundamental economic change than whether people identify as "liberal" or "conservative". 29% of conservative Republicans, and 49% of conservative to moderate Democrats respond **negatively** to the word "capitalism". 46% of liberal Democrats respond **positively** to the word "capitalism" (Pew, 12-28-11). "Liberal" is very often about social issues, not economic ones, and many liberals have college degrees and are affluent. Many conservatives are working class. These are even stereotypes.

What it will take to win

"Evils which are patiently endured when they seem inevitable become intolerable once the idea of escape from them is suggested. " - de Tocqueville (from The Economist, 5-10-14, pg. 55)

We can't know what event or spark might finally begin to wake people out of the learned helplessness and demoralization that now pervades America's "middle class" (working class). Occupy, started by anarchists, did this for a time. People will probably need a better sense of what to do before acting in a sustained way. Right from the start, our projects need to be practical and empowering. ("Empowerment" is an ironically overused word in a "society" where most people tolerate abject powerlessness.) We need to be decentralized, innovative, fluid, and unpredictable. Refer to earlier chapters: 11. Death Panels for Capitalism and 19. Transitional Economics: Where Working People are Taking Power Now for more on this.

Coupled with a deep vision, and especially a deep spiritual foundation, this can build a virtuous cycle that reverses the current vicious cycle of demoralization and decline.

Working people need to start thinking like masters instead of slaves. Even making demands is the behavior of uppity slaves. Free workers simply create what they want, and create/find the resources and power to do so.

Vision has to be reality-based. People are so demoralized now that giddy "Revolution-Around-the-Corner" fantasies are hard to even imagine. But initial success could change that. A far more watered-down version of giddy, weak-minded thinking was the Obamania that swept America in 2008 and the first half of 2009, especially among the young. I just rolled my eyes. How could people be so gullable? The double-talk about globalization in Obama's book, and all the Wall St. $$$ he was getting was all I needed to know.

166

Along the same lines, any movement dependent on a few charismatic leaders is extremely vulnerable. These leaders can be taken out, as a number were in the '60's, if they can't be corrupted or set-up. Centralization makes a movement very easy to infiltrate and destroy. The police state, and the parallel private apparatus hired directly by the wealthy, will have vast resources at their disposal. But we will have growing numbers, and from this not inconsiderable resources of our own.

Some quotes from our police-state friends are instructive:

"Some applauded the Animal Liberation Front's efforts; others condemned them. But the FBI wasn't able to contain these tofu-eating activists. The more aggressively the ALF was pursued, the more easily it recruited new members. Like AA, the ALF lacked formal leadership, top-down hierarchy and structure. It was just a loose collection of informal circles linked by common beliefs. But its seemingly chaotic structure made it incredibly resilient to attack. The ALF drew its power from its decentralization.

Back in the 1580's, the Spanish were the ones surprised by the power of a seemingly chaotic starfish enemy. They had easily conquered the Aztecs and Incas – impressive civilizations with elaborate infrastructure and strong leadership. But now the Spanish encountered the Apaches. For 200 years, the Apaches withstood Spanish (and later Mexican and American) attacks. Unlike the Aztecs or Incas, the Apaches were a distributed society. Instead of cities, they had small villages; instead of formal structure, loosely connected groups. Instead of powerful chiefs, they had Nant'ans (the most famous of whom was Geronimo), who led by **example**. When the Spanish burned a village, the Apaches moved on; when they killed a Nant'an, another tribe member would take his place. The harder the Spanish attacked, the more decentralized – and resilient – the Apaches became."

"Centralize the opponent. Why did the Apaches finally lose, after two centuries of independence and insurrection? As compensation for moving to reservations, the Americans gave the Nant'ans cows to distribute among the tribe. With this scarce resource came real, as opposed to symbolic, power.

As a result, the Apaches became more centralized, and therefore much easier to control." (from "The 'starfish model' for the war on terrorism", Ori Brafman and Rod A. Beckstrom, in the S.F. Chronicle, 9-15-06)

War may seem a dire analogy, but we **already** live in a class war. It just isn't a shooting war (at least yet). If the grip of the wealthy 1% on America is ever seriously threatened, even by completely non-violent non-obedience, this oligarchy will make little distinction between my book and an al-Qaeda website (1). We will see just how little "rule of law" America really has. Greed is an addiction, a disease. It rewires the brain just like alcohol/drug addiction.

The backbone (and **mind**) of an emerging free working class in America has to be a decentralized network of small, face-to-face groups based in our workplaces and neighborhoods. These organic groups are much harder to infiltrate and destroy, **especially** when they become numerous. They also keep power **directly** in the hands of working people.

The most advanced of these will be worker-owned/self-managed enterprises and allied property forms. In a full-blown depression, collective self-help and neighborhood assemblies will be more pressing projects. The advanced layer attaining self-management capacity will be a growing **functional** vanguard, spreading the **practical** capacity for working-class power. A merely ideological "vanguard", spouting Politically Correct Lines, will not even begin to cut it. Overall, these small, organic groups will exchange/spread **experiential** expertise and information. This body of practical knowhow will grow as the groups become more numerous. An iron law: The more widely distributed self-organization/self-management capacity is, the more powerful and free working people will be. And the more indestructible our power/freedom becomes.

Any needed self-defense capacity can rise quickly out of this already growing self-organization. Any plan to violently crush uppity American workers will face an inconvenient fact: **millions** of us **already have** serious firepower. Asymetrical/irregular war is a skill-set that will need to be as widely distributed as possible. Paradoxically, this is exactly what can make a full-blown shooting war unnecessary. This has been called deterrence/ peace thru strength.

The Army will be an unreliable tool for a police state, and my guess is that it will be used conservatively. Most GI's come from the working class, and did not sign up to grind the heel of a boot in the faces of American working people. There is even an organization called Oath Keepers working to prevent this. It claimed 8000 members in 2012, but it is also led by a right-wing libertarian.

The real dirty-work of repression would be carried out by the police state itself (FBI, NSA, CIA, ect.) and its various tentacles in local police departments. Even more – by a parallel private apparatus hired directly by the wealthy. (The private sector is **so** much more efficient . . .)

If the capitalist oligarchy wants a violent revolution or a protracted civil war, violent repression is the quickest way to git one. For examples, see Nicaragua and El Salvador (1978-1992). Here in the U.S.A., Occupy Oakland exploded after Scott Olsen, a Marine vet with 2 tours of duty in Iraq, was shot in the head by police and nearly killed. 40,000 people showed up on a work day to shut down the financial district and the Port of Oakland.

Pinochet, the butcher/torture-master of Chile (and Margret Thatcher's faithful lap-dog) was able to do his thing in the 1970's because the Chilean people were helpless. Nobody had guns or were able to get them. That is **far** from the case here in America, and the capitalist oligarchy knows this.

To generalize, the basic operating principles of libertarian working-class self-organization are as follows:

1. Free association
2. Voluntary co-operation
3. Direct action
4. Self-management
5. Mutual aid
6. Self-defense

(1) This oligarchy would in fact **vastly** prefer an al-Qaeda website to something like my book ever going big. Al-Qaeda was such a **useful** enemy between 2001 and 2004, distracting people from our real problems. Some even claim the CIA created it.

Race War: The final trump-card of a threatened oligarchy

WHY go through all the fuss (and mess) of trying to crush American workers as a bloc, when it's SO much easier to get us to fight each other? The capitalist crisis has already raised racial tensions as well as class consciousness. Consider a telling passage from The Economist (12-7-13), from an article titled Why Americans are so angry:

"Now almost two-thirds say others cannot be trusted, a record high." "Consider the crisis around Obamacare. . . . The president's headache is that voters see his plan as welfare for the poor rather than a better way of delivering medical care. That is exposing ugly divisions. Most starkly, a majority of whites think the law will make life worse for them, a National Journal poll found, while most non-whites believe it will help people like them. . . . This is America's real problem with trust. The country faces a crisis of mutual resentment, masquerading as a general collapse in national morale. Sharply-delineated voter blocs are alarmingly willing to believe that rival groups are up to no good or taking more than their fair share."

In fact, Obamacare really IS mostly a redistribution of income **within** the bottom 90% of Americans. 40% of us (under age 65) will get seriously subsidized or even free healthcare, including around 55% of the working class. These people are disproportionately Latino and black. 40% of us (under age 65) will get gouged even **worse** than we already are to pay for this, including around 25% of the working class. These people are disproportionately white. Meanwhile, the U.S. Healthcare Fraud and Extortion Racket grinds on as before. All these dues subsidies merely subsidize the Chargemaster, as Chargemaster rates are built in to health insurance premiums (see Chapter 9 of this book). This is because the U.S. Healthcare Fraud and Extortion Racket **dictated** to the Obama administration what the allowed parameters of the Affordable Care Act would be. There is a small tax increase, about 1.7% (excluding capital-gains income), on the truly rich (the top 2.5%) to help pay for this mess.

U.S. liberalism has been doing this kind of thing since the late 1960's. It is not really progressive. It is elitist, coercive social-engineering that working-class Americans pay for, leaving the powerful wealthy barely touched. And it **pits** working people against each other. This may even be its intent. Affirmative-action quotas and forced busing have done every bit as much to inflame racial tensions as the much-discussed coded racism of Republicans.

Even the widely popular Social Security and Medicare programs are paid for by absolutely regressive taxes (Social Security) or effectively regressive taxes (Medicare). They merely redistribute income from under age 65 working-class people to over age 65 working-class people. The wealthy barely pay for any of it. (1)

Even using genuinely progressive taxes to recover some of the wealth/income the rich have gouged out of us is only band-aid therapy. It does not **end** the theft at its source, and can be gutted with loopholes or rolled-back outright at any time, as it **always** has been.

U.S. liberalism has been so discredited with voters that its politicians run from the word, preferring the word "progressive". If U.S. "progressives" do not face and rectify their fundamental **class** problem, they have **no** business wondering why so many of the working people they claim to champion refuse to vote for them.

Historical U.S. racism

None of the above is to deny that white racism in particular is a crippling problem within the American working class. I have included this subchapter for historical context.

As mentioned in the redneck chapter, it is a lie that the Civil War ended the enslavement of blacks. Not only (with a few exceptions) did blacks

never get the repatriation of 40 acres and a mule they were promised, black Union troops were systematically disarmed, and blacks were **never** allowed remotely enough firepower to defend themselves against resurgent white-supremacist terror. Not only was the slave-owning oligarchy allowed to keep all its ill-gotten land, and re-enslave blacks in new forms, there was never any Nuremburg Trial to hold them accountable for the monstrous crimes they committed during outright slave-ownership. I have seen a photo of a black guy who's entire back was covered solid with deep, mangled scar tissue from repeated torture.

And there was more to come. The Supreme Court's Cruikshank decision in 1876 enabled blacks to be totally stripped of any ability to defend themselves. They were forced to watch helplessly as thousands of lynchings ground on over decades. Victims were commonly tortured or burned to death. "The men and women who tortured, dismembered, and murdered in this fashion understood perfectly well what they were doing and thought of themselves as perfectly normal human beings. Few had any ethical qualms about their actions. . . . One has only to view the self-satisfied expressions on their faces . . . What is most disturbing about these scenes is the discovery that the perpetrators of these crimes were ordinary people, not so different from ourselves – merchants, farmers, laborers, machine operators, teachers, doctors, lawyers, policemen, students; they were family men and women, good churchgoing folk, who came to believe that keeping black people in their place was nothing less than pest control . . ." (Leon F. Litwack, Without Sanctuary, 2000). "Even the Nazis did not stoop to selling souvenirs of Auschwitz, but lynching scenes became a burgeoning subdepartment of the postcard industry." (Time, 4-2-00) No Nuremberg Trial for these monsters either.

Leon Litwacks's account of the number of black people lynched from 1882 to 1968 is 4742. The Tuskegee Institute (1979): 3335. Both are probably conservative. The geographic breakdown of these atrocities should be noted: Deep South (SC, GA, FL, AL, MS, LA, AR, TX) plus TN: 2860. "Border" South (KY, NC, VA, WV, MD, OK): 475. By chronology:

1882-88: 440, 1889-1903: 1585, 1904-1922: 1143, 1923-1935: 213, 1936-1946: 50, 1947-1964: 14, 1965-68: 0. (Tuskegee Institute, 1979)

The biggest response by blacks to this endless train of abominations was to leave land they had lived on for one to two centuries. More than 1.5 million went North between 1910 and 1940. In 1919, during a deep recession compounded by WWI vets returning home and looking for jobs, there was a wave of white attacks on blacks across the industrial North. Most of the attackers were white immigrants or first-generation whites competing for scarce jobs. The outcome here was **very** different than in the South. Blacks had the firepower to defend themselves and the white attackers took heavy casualties. The attacks stopped **immediately**. One ugly exception in the South was the Tulsa, Oklahoma pogrom of 1921. Blacks were very poorly armed, and up to 300 were killed. 37 city blocks were burned to the ground, and 10,000 blacks made homeless.

Two redneck movements around this period should be noted. The populist movement from 1890 on spread all over the Midwest, West, and South. In the South, it initially tried to unite black and white working people. It then came under vicious, well-funded attack from the Southern Democratic Party machine, in great part as "nigger-lovers". In response, the Southern populists split, with a majority led by Tom Watson turning on blacks; the non-racist minority was smashed. Later, in the 1930's, a populist movement led by Huey Long won power in Louisiana. It was no champion of civil rights, but neither did it play the race card.

One more ugly historical footnote: Upon returning from combat in WW2, black vets were cut out of the GI Bill given to whites (scholarships for college, low-interest and lower down-payment home loans) (N.Y. Times, 8-28-05). I think Truman changed this when the military was integrated in the 1950's, but I'm not sure. Blacks who did attempt to become homeowners were subjected to vicious loan sharking (and redlining) by capitalist banks throughout the post-war boom, which denied them any effective rights as homeowners (Atlantic, 5-21-14). This was not effectively challenged until the late 1960's.

"Rednecks for Obama"

The geographic breakdown of historic racist atrocities can be compared to recent white voting patterns. To repeat myself, I had no illusions about Obama, but I wanted to know how many rednecks in 2008 would vote for a black president who at least claimed to be concerned about the issues facing working people.

What I found was that whites in the South "enlightened" with at least a 4-year college degree were **no** more willing to vote for Obama than those **terrible** working-class rednecks. And a lot of those terrible rednecks **were** willing to vote for Obama: 30% to 41% in the "border" South and Florida, and 44% to 53% of working-class whites in Midwest states with a large redneck population (OH, IN, MI, IL). Only in the remnant core of the Deep South did the redneck vote for Obama get really low: 9% to 11% in AL, MI, LA, somewhat less low at 21% to 26% in TX, GA, SC. The college-degree'd vote was **no** different in most of these states. What is striking about the sizable redneck vote for Obama in the "border" South states is that 5 out of 8 of these states were not even seriously contested by the Obama campaign. There was, however, an independent "Rednecks for Obama" website that got millions of hits.

Redneck culture has two different historical rivers. Starting with vast land grants from the English king, the slave-owning oligarchy took nearly all the rich, black alluvial bottomland. A minority of rednecks became enmeshed in this slave economy as overseers/whippers, escaped slave hunters, and other service-providers, plus peripheral sharecroppers, tenant-farmers, and small freeholders. The hilly to mountainous red land, starting with Appillachia, was poorer and the slave-owning oligarchy did not want it. So it was left to real-estate speculators and the great majority of rednecks, who had no involvement in the slave economy. Many of these redneck counties, stretching clear into Northern Georgia and Alabama, refused to vote for succession at the outbreak of the Civil War. Over 150 years later, we can still see a major difference in redneck voting patterns.

Quotas vs. reparations

Returning to the first subchapter, a question: What, exactly, does an affirmative-action quota get a black person today? Chosen instead of a white working-class person for a precarious job, under an exploiter, which could vanish at any time without warning. With technology and offshoring, capitalism is going to be destroying a lot more jobs than it creates for a long time. Even this assumes we don't get a full-blown depression, which could start at any time. The capitalist oligarchy is **more** than happy to accommodate demands for affirmative-action quotas. Working people pay for them, and they get us squabbling over a shrinking pile of crumbs.

Reparations would look like this: land, housing, productive assets, educational opportunities and technical assistance. The wealthy oligarchy, especially the decendents of the slave-owning oligarchy, would pay for it, not other working people. Not only would this actually rectify racial injustice, it would create **class emancipation**. As of 2010, the median net worth of a black household was all of $5677.

As for Politically Correct Identity Politics, it gets worse. Wealthy immigrants from China, India, and Arab oil sheikdoms must get included in quotas at universities, because they are "People of Color". Poor rednecks should **not**, because they have "white skin privelage". "Aspirational" white yuppie women whine about glass ceilings and how men still run the world, while bossing around their Latina housekeepers (yuppies are **busy** people, and everything has to be just so). White gay male yuppies push working-class families, many of them black and Latino, out of any neighborhood they choose to gentrify, while whining about all the terrible homophobia. We can now move on to the patriarchal slights endured by the heiresses of grand fortunes. And a gay heir to a grand fortune was **snubbed** by someone at a 5-star catered affair!

The underclass: racialization of a CLASS issue

We have all heard, for years on end, about "black crime" and the "black underclass", more recently "Mexican gangs". Everyone has heard about the well-documented racial profiling by police and others. Many readers will be too young to remember the infamous Willie Horton attack-ads that George Bush the 1ˢᵗ ran in his successful 1988 presidential campaign. Very recently, Paul Ryan (mastermind of that plot to privatize Medicare and sic the Chargemaster on the over 65 set) was making references to the attitudes of the "inner-city poor" in presentations. As everyone knows, this is code for "black". **Expert** on poverty that he fancies himself (having grown up with 20 silver spoons in his mouth), Paul Ryan somehow failed to notice that the % of rural people below the federal poverty line (2) is almost exactly the same as for urban people.

The Marxist term for underclass is lumpen, and this class is **not** to be confused with the working poor. This class includes the people we've all heard so much about: chronic welfare dependents, drug dealers, pimps and gang members, drug-addicted thieves, mentally ill and/or drug/alcohol addicted homeless. America, with by far the worst maldistribution of wealth and income of any "developed" country, has the added "benefit" from this of an unusually large (and growing) underclass.

As should be obvious to anyone, underclass comes in **all** colors. My particular ethnic group, redneck, is easily up to 15% underclass. The black % is higher, over 20%, for historical reasons I've highlighted earlier in this chapter. Growing up in the highly chaotic, violent, and (unless drug money is abundant) impoverished underclass "life" is **highly** destructive to normal human brain/character development, even by the debased standards of Late Capitalism. And as should be obvious to anyone, white lumpen grow up to exhibit exactly the same dysfunctional, antisocial, and violent behavior as black lumpen. Only the mood-music and style of attire is different. And if you compared **working class** rednecks to **working class** blacks, you might well find a higher rate of violence among the rednecks. (This too is a stereotype, ethnic profiling if you will.)

The underclass/lumpen, not being working-class, do not have class consciousness, except often as being lower class. They do tend to have, however, a **lot** of **race** consciousness, all too often of an exceedingly stupid kind. Anyone fancying the delusion that white lumpen are any different should note that prison is by far the No. 1 recruiting-ground for white-supremacist outfits. The underclass/lumpen, of **all** 3 major U.S. races, will be the #1 tool used for attempts to forment a full-blown race war in America.

The "radicals"/left-liberals who romanticize the underclass (**only**, however, if they are "People of Color") are usually young upper-middle-class whites sheltered from any real exposure to it. Working-class people can afford no such illusions. We know our neighborhoods can be turned into violent, crime-ridden slums at any time, an especially large concern if we have kids or are old. And we are in at least as much danger of this if we are black or Latino as if we are white. This in fact happened to my Dad's neighborhood when he was retired.

Now in some urban neighborhoods, a new class-plague is being visited upon us. Swarms of yuppies, bored to tears with tony suburbs, now want the stimulation of the big city. And so, with the bone-crushing rents they bring, they drive out the very "ethnic" working-class people, artists, musicians, and writers who made these places interesting in the first place. (This is, of course, a huge boon to working-class people fortunate enough to be homeowners.)

The only hope for the underclass is to totally break with that "life" and culture. I have met people (most of them black) who have actually done this. The working class will not have the considerable power/resources needed to help enable this until we are **in** power. This will need to be facilitated by ex-lumpen who know first- hand the kind of damage growing up like that produces, and what it takes to overcome it. We will not need or want any "help" from a spoiled, ignorant princeling like Paul Ryan. It should be emphasized here that the **younger** this break is enabled, the better – early childhood if possible. Even before he is born, an underclass kid is being damaged by constant elevated stress hormones in the mother, from the surrounding chaos and violence, usually with added help from a junk-food diet (slums are notorious "food deserts"). Never mind even more help from alcohol/drug abuse.

The underclass/lumpen issue is going to have a huge added twist as the deepening slavery of Late Capitalism grinds on. As capitalism destroys far more jobs than it creates, with technology and offshoring, many millions more once-solidly working class people are going to join the chronically unemployed. This will happen even without a full-blown depression, and has in fact already been underway since 2008. As has been noted by many others, the labor force has been shrinking by millions since 2008, and had that not occurred, the unemployment rate in 2013 would be at least 11%, not the 7% of official statistics.

Looking ahead . . .

If working people are successfully rising up together, the danger of race war will recede. When we were doing this in the industrial Midwest in 1936-37, attempts to forment racial division made some headway, but failed. Unity will be **greatly** facilitated if right from the start, the various racial/ethnic subtribes of the vast American working-class supertribe sit down together and hash out our issues. James Webb (author of Born Fighting, cited at the start of this book) has long called for blacks and rednecks to sit down together. This should obviously be extended to the other major working-class subtribes such as Latinos and "ethnic" whites (Poles, Italians, Catholic Irish) who's ancestors arrived in America more recently than rednecks. (Rednecks are "ethnic" whites too, we've just been here for 300 years.)

The danger of race war rises if rising working people make serious strategic or tactical errors and are defeated. The danger rises much more if working people fail to rise up at all. This last scenario will mean America is in terminal decline as a culture.

In this last scenario, the racial and cultural divisions that have been festering since the late 1960's will greatly worsen. For decades, when people have moved, they have been self-sorting into "blue" and "red" areas, and this has been accelerating. America has been polarizing into two separate countries. Again, this is mostly around racial and cultural issues – "blue" states actually have **worse** economic inequality than "red" states. California, for all its much ballyhooed cultural liberalism, has a larger percentage of its people living in **real** poverty (when real living costs – like housing and healthcare are taken into account) than **any** "red" state – even the much-maligned Mississippi (3). Welcome to the Politically Correct Liberal Plantation! In a disintegrating America in terminal decline, **none** of its fragments are going to be nice places for working people to live. We can add to this mess creeping (or not so creeping) repression – including of the Politically Correct Liberal variety in many "blue" states.

A related result of the failure to rise up is the relentless increase of petty interpersonal meanness and violence. There are 1.8 million acts of physical violence in the workplace every year (Labor Dept.), and 26% of workers quit their job because of bullying or incivility at work (2011, Civility in America). I don't have a breakdown of what portion of this is between bosses and workers, and what portion is between co-workers. Instead of rising together against a system that relentlessly degrades us, people take it out on each other. Unless this changes, it will only get much worse.

For working people, the real-life consequences of failing to self-organize and solve our problems will get increasingly ugly.

(1) One factor that soured many working people on liberalism was the bracket-creep of the graduated income tax during the inflationary 1973-1981 period. Income tax brackets were **never** indexed to inflation during this period, when Democratic Party politicians had **every** opportunity to do this from 1975 to 1980. Reagan,

of all people, finally did this in 1981, with a working majority at the time in Congress. Add to this endlessly rising crime and declining real wages during this period. From 1977 to 1980, rapidly rising housing prices also greatly helped make Reagan's siren-song appealing to working-class homeowners.

(2) The Federal poverty line is a useless and dishonest statistic. It is only a multiple of food costs, with **no** accounting for housing and healthcare costs, which have risen much faster.

(3) The Census Bureau in 2011 introduced a more honest poverty measure that considers both govt. benefits and real living costs like housing, healthcare, transportation, and childcare in any given region. For states, California came in dead worst with 25% of its people unable to provide for basic necessities. (N.Y. Times, 5-10-14)

Commentary on the Spanish and Russian revolutions

A strict, literal translation of anarchy (a Greek word) is no rule – i.e. true communism or classless and stateless society. But working people can only lay the foundation for this by taking complete power.

Where the Catalan/Aragon workers and peasants **wanted** to take power – over our workplaces, land, and neighborhoods – we did so, brilliantly. We even took over society-wide infrastructure – water, electricity, public transit – brilliantly. Self-management was our Holy Grail for 3 generations, and when the time came (Franco's attempted fascist takeover in 1936), we rose to the occasion. Brilliantly.

But we displayed an abject failure of social will when it came to destroying the pitiful remnants of the State in July/Aug. of 1936, when we easily had the power to do so. Here we did **not** behave like good anarchists.

The next task was taking Saragossa, with its arms industry, enabling the arming of the **entire** working class, with little or no dependence on Stalin and his cronies in the Republican State. We had already taken over a Ford plant in Barcelona, and were retooling it to make armored cars and tanks.

The only "Red Army" that will be allowed by a free working class will be the **entire** armed working class itself. And **that**, my friends, is from Lenin's State and Revolution (1917). Too bad he betrayed this libertarian promise with war communism. Any attempt to create a special body of armed men (and this phrase is straight out of State and Revolution) will be destroyed – at gunpoint. This even echoes the American Revolution's dread of a Standing Army – enshrined in our Constitution's 2nd Amendment.

Necessary society-wide coordination will be facilitated (**not** dictated) by elected, recallable delegates – along the lines of the Aragon Council. This council would have **no** Standing Army to force edicts (**unlike** the Bolshevik party bosses under war communism). It will lead only thru expertise and persuasion. Anarchist workers in Catalonia were willing, against their best instincts, to follow **bad** advice from CNT "leaders" who had joined the capitalist/Stalinist Republican State. I'd imagine they'd be far more willing to follow advice from elected/recallable delegates that were serious about working class rule. The precursor to this was the Aragon Council, and how well Catalan workers self-managed / coordinated armed self-defense and necessary society-wide infrastructure.

Anarchists need to come clean about our fatal abject failure to destroy the State (i.e. behave like good anarchists) when we easily had the power to do so.

Leninists need to come clean about the abject, fatal, self-inflicted disaster of war communism (during the Russian civil war) – led by Lenin and Trotsky. The militarization of labor (the **exact** opposite of self-management) was the direct precursor to the vicious hyper-exploitation of workers under Stalin. The forced requisitioning from peasants was the direct precursor to the forced collectivization of peasants under Stalin – which was genocidal and permanently crippled Russian agriculture. The Cheka was the direct precursor to the KGB and gulag. A near-totalitarian one-party State, that did not even allow factions within it, was a direct precursor to the fully totalitarian, show trial Stalinist State. A centralized machine of "Professional Revolutionaries", heavily implanted from **outside** the working class (see Lenin's What Is To Be Done (1903) for exciting details – Lenin himself was a child of the well-to-do, unlike Durruti) was the direct precursor to nomenklatura rule – a **class enemy** helped greatly by the Lenin levy/implantation of Tsarist bureaucrats. And this was the direct precursor to the nomenclatura capitalism that Russia and China now have (see Orwell's Animal Farm for exciting prophetic details).

Nearly ALL of the foundations of Stalinism, and finally nomenklatura capitalism, were directly laid by war communism. Trotsky was murdered by the monster he helped create, along with at least 10 million other Russians, including most of the original Bolsheviks.

It is worth noting here that the voluntary, self-managed peasant collectives of Aragon, in alliance with the Catalan workers, under conditions of civil war, raised agricultural production 20% in a single year (see Anthony Beevor's The Battle for Spain – also for a good summary of industrial self-management, see also The Anarchists Collectives, edited by Sam Dolgoff).

To sum up: free workers need to use ideologies practically as tool kits – use what works and chuck the rest. Lenin has lots of helpful things to say in State and Revolution, and I personally know Leninists who have contributed well to the emancipation of my People. We do not need to throw out anarchist or Leninist babies with their baskets.

Back to our present situation in America. The majority of American workers have begun to face the fact that we have allowed ourselves to be made into slaves. But most of us have become so dependent on employers for a livelihood, on being managed, that it would now be hard for most of us to self-manage ourselves out of a paper bag. But there is a fundamental contradiction here – the development of the productive base requires many more of us to be more skilled – and so more capable of self-management. And this, my friends, is the functional opening wedge for working-class power right here in America.

Postscript:

Discussing these questions with a Trotskyist friend of mine (of 36 years), he said: " War communism destroyed communism. But what you have to answer here is what (anarchists) would do instead, given the objective conditions. Not some fantasy wish-list, but given the objective conditions that actually existed."

I have begun to answer this necessary question in this brief essay. This job needs to be finished. It should be noted here that the objective conditions facing anarchist Spain were not very different than what Bolshevik Russia faced during their civil war. We had a 3-cornered civil war in which well-armed fascists, Stalinists, and liberal capitalists, with generous support from Hitler and Stalin, were determined to strangle a newborn free working class in its cradle. And as if that wasn't enough – a blockade plus a capital strike from the liberal capitalist powers (even France under the Socialist-led Popular Front), who we foolishly hoped would come to our aid (1). We had almost NO outside support, and woefully inadequate firepower for the tasks at hand.

A 2nd necessary note, concerning the productive base. In 1936, Catalan workers in every enterprise decided what they wanted/were able to do. 80% of industry was taken over and run by the workers. The remainder had worker's councils co-existing with capitalist management, or remained under capitalist rule. A precursor to this was the 100,000 Catalan workers who had started and built worker-owned, self-managed enterprises before 1936, under bad conditions (experiential expertise – again see Anthony Beevor). Remnant, marginalized, freely chosen capitalism inside Free Catalonia was **no** real threat to working-class freedom. The **real** threat came from outside. Self-management organically crowds-out capitalism, **far** more effectively than ham-handed attempts to ban it from above by a State (which only creates a black market greatly helped by State corruption – a precursor to nomenklatura capitalism). Bureaucrats are pathetically predictable.

Back to America now. Real working-class power here will have distinctly American characteristics. It will be decentralized, flexible, self-managed/innovative/entrepreneurial, and from this, libertarian. Well –fitting our actually existing productive base. Americans do **not** like heavy-handed government. Far less forced collectivism imposed by a near-totalitarian war communist State. (Never mind how pathetically ill fitted to our actually existing productive base this monstrosity would be.) Any attempt to impose war communism on America would be such an abjectly pathetic suicide-march that it does not even deserve **any** serious discussion.

Some helpful slogans/memes for America's 99%'ers:

Free the Working Class 200 Million.

END Capitalist Rule.

DIRECT Power to Working People.

Co-operatives – the Rule of Labor Over Capital.

It is time to put real working-class power on the American agenda.

FOOTNOTES:

1. It should be noted here that the rulers of Britain and France paid dearly for their treachery. Hitler overran France and pounded the shit out of Britain. Had these dear liberal fools seriously helped to stop Hitler in Spain, it would at least have bought them more time to prepare for the **inevitable** World War 2.0. What goes around comes around.

Re: "Is income inequality a bad thing?"
(S.F. Chronicle Open Forum, 10-14-13)

I have to agree with the slavery apologists of the Hoover Institute on one point: "First, is it really the role of government to equalize Americans personal income?" No it isn't. We working people have to do this ourselves. And the point here isn't to make everyone get the same income. It is to enable working people to keep the wealth we create.

I just read an article about workers fleeing crushing housing costs in the Silicon Valley/S.F. Bay Area. They are moving to the far outer fringes, in the San Joaquin Valley, where they endure 4 **hours** of commuting every day, in the slow-motion, twice-a-day mass cattle run. (And this has been going on here as far back as the late 1980's.) We are allowing ourselves to be reduced to **livestock** for the wealthy, here to feed their monstrous addiction. This individual "solution" to housing extortion is **no** solution at all, and inflicts great hardship on those who attempt it. A mass rent and mortgage strike would **shut down** this extortion racket in a hurry, at far less cost to its victims, but people have to **do it**.

Likewise, widespread irregular/unpredictable strikes at work, including occupations, and mass, protracted shutdowns of Wall St./K St., would **far** more effectively jam the machinery of our deepening enslavement than whining for the government to do something about it. Even any government action on this problem, as ham-handed and ineffectual as it may be, is **far** more likely if we actually **do** something.

An Iron Law of this "society" is as follows: We will be subjected to **exactly** as much slavery and extortion as we are willing to tolerate. (This is paraphrased from Frederick Douglass.)

Everyone is for "freedom". Freedom for **which** class? In a worker-owned/self-managed enterprise, workers keep **all** the wealth we create and capitalist parasites to not even have the freedom to exist. Government has nothing to do with this. If you aspire to be a capitalist – i.e. suck on wealth other people create – and feel this is Gulag, you don't have to join an enterprise of this kind.

Then there are all the other capitalist parasites: gouging landlords, bone-crushing mortgages, credit-card debt (at 12% - 26% interest), student loans, and finally, the U.S. Healthcare Fraud and Extortion Racket (see Time magazine expose, 3-4-13).

In my case, having gotten rid of all these too (or never having allowed them in the first place), I now live in that Totalitarian Horror – the Worker's Paradise (gasp!).

Closing remarks

Obscene income inequality is a "hot topic" that is not going away ANYTIME soon. My very brief commentary on the squalid, dishonest Hoover Institution editorial only deals with transitional economics, not the full Return.

The full Return will sound wildly Utopian to most Americans: "Full regeneration of normal human life/intimacy with the rest of nature. . . . What is now called 'mystical experience' will be universal and frequent. Quality of life so deep as to be unimaginable to most humans alive today." (from a core chapter in my book) For me, this is not imagination. I have actually had this level of experience.

And now, from the sublime to the ridiculous: the Left. I recently read an article in the Nation about the emerging Left challenge to Obama. Its agenda was such stale, bleached pablum that I can't imagine anyone being inspired by it, or even interested.

Stalinism/Maoism is not and never will be a real issue in America. Our real choices are: 1. "Free market" neo-liberalism (starting with Reagan) and its barely distinguishable "New Democrat" sibling (starting with

Clinton). 2. Shallow, tired, has-been Progressivism (Americanese for Social Democracy). 3. Anarchism. Which is to say there is really only one choice.

People are only inspired to DO something (in a sustained way) when they have vision. Few Americans identify as anarchist, or even have a clue what it means. (When it emerges as a real force here, de-facto anarchism may get called something like "Left Libertarianism".) But there are tens of millions of Americans who are revolted by the "society" we are "living" in. They just don't know how we got like this or what to do about it. Far less what is possible (and necessary). I hope to God my book can reach some of them.

BAD KITTY

A Journal of Terrorist Lifestyles

Spring 2008

Howard and Dorothy Smith's cougar, Big Joe. (Photo by Dorothy Smith, courtesy of Lyn Hancock)

The 220 lb. lap cat. NO cage or chain for THIS kitty.

For free humans and the free cougars who choose to live with them.

Heeere kitty, kitty, kitty . . .
Such a BAAAD kitty!

Lynn and Bart have lived with cougars for 25 years.
They aren't able to let their cougars run free,
But the cougars have a 6 acre enclosure to themselves.

Excerpt from letter from Bart Culver
(Bart has lived with cougars for 25 years)

I will devote the rest of this letter to the idea of trusting cougars. They are capable of love. They seem incapable of deceit. But they think one thought at a time, intensely. They love intensely. But if, for just one second, they get mad at you as any human who loves you could be expected to do, then their strength and their bite pressure is awesome. One expression of anger which would do no lasting harm to another cougar (say, a sibling or a mother) would inflict grievous wounds on you, and bring out a defensive reaction that could trigger a killing attack. Another cougar would growl back, slap back, and stave off the attack. No human being has any type of combat skills that would not seem pitiful to a cougar.

"Keep your eyes on the cat" really is about knowing the cat's state of mind and avoiding any acts of mischieviousness or anger. You are asking more of a cougar companion than you are of a human. NEVER get angry at me. NEVER mistreat me. NEVER take advantage of your strength. NEVER resent or misunderstand anything I do. Although I am INFERIOR, always respect me like a god. Not every cougar can be trusted to always be this extraordinary. It takes a special cat, and a very special all-consuming relationship.

Yes, I have had such a relationship, and no, there are not many people who could do it. You would have to select a kitten/kittens from a long line of super sweeties, bottle feed and sleep with them from the time their eyes open. Probably hunt with a bow with them and give them food, and still, as able hunters, they may not share a kill with you (I never tried that). I HAVE had cougars get angry at me and pantomime an attack, exercising self-restraint. I am very grateful for that, and very proud. I consider that beyond a reasonable expectation. You can only gentle a functioning carnivore so much before you are in the realm of miracles. And how many miracles do any of us deserve?

Yours,

Bart

Feline Filial Love
By Bart Culver

I have been a scientist and thoroughly enjoyed the thrill of discovery, yet there are some mysteries I wish science could never unravel. Like love. How wonderful will love be when science reduces it to a series of equations – when there are chemicals that can make anyone fall in or out of love at any time? We are just about there. Pandora's box is open wide. We have no choice now but to peer inside, try not to arouse the demons, and search for seeds of wisdom. Here's one – objective information of our direct experience that animals can love.

Several studies have been done where people in love were shown pictures of their beloved while their brain activity was observed by magnetic resonance imaging. These studies revealed that human love is part of a reward system originating in the sub-cortex, which is common to all mammalian brains. The formation of "attachments" occurs in the dopamine circuit of the limbic system. Stimulation of dopamine and ocytocin receptors produces mating and bonding behaviors in mammalian species from rhesus monkeys to voles. This is a mammalian survival mechanism that scientists describe as "empathic resonance" or "limbic resonance".

Basically, science has found no evidence that mammals cannot love. Instead, it has shown that all mammals possess all the equipment humans use to love. From this I conclude that the most reasonable explanation for why animals behave as though they love us is that they do. Of course, we cannot expect animal love and human love always to have the same behavioral manifestations. That is precluded by many obvious differences in comprehension, communication, perception, and social modalities. Compared to humans, animals have crude language and simple rules of social interaction. But they have vastly superior olfactory sensitivity to the physical and emotional status of others. When I visit my feline friends, they feel obliged to present their posteriors to me. They are offering me a wealth of information I am incapable of receiving. Yet they assume I now have this information. They could well be confused or offended by my failure to reciprocate. Human sensory deficiencies create so many opportunities for interspecies misunderstandings that our success in routinely avoiding them is quite remarkable. I find two explanations for this: operant conditioning and trust born of love. I have experimented with operant conditioning of three bottle-raised cougars, where the only reward was praise and affection, and all three learned to jump across three pedestals through a hula-hoop in one afternoon. They initiated this training by sitting at my feet, waiting for me to teach them something, as their mother would normally do. Their survival depends on learning, which requires their brains to be programmed to pay close attention to their mother and desire her approval. You could call this programming instinct, or you could be more precise and call it filial love. And although it may have begun with the awareness that their mother is the source of food and all good things, it obviously transcends food rewards. In fact, it is not necessary for infants to love their mothers to be fed. It is only necessary for the mother to love them. That leaves us with learning as the primary reward for filial love, and love as the essential prerequisite for learning.

It is ridiculous for people to postulate that animals are playing you – pretending to love you – for food. What? They understand love, but do not love? They're all psychopaths? Nonsense. And what of the mother's love? The perpetuation of her genes is the reward for her love. But for her to be aware of that would require knowledge and a cerebral hemisphere beyond what she has. So, like all human mothers, she is aware that her children are part of her, they are her life's work, and she loves them. As animal caregivers, we give or at least mimic maternal love and receive filial love. Have you ever noticed that for adolescents and adults, it is not the one who is feeding them now, but the one who fed them as an infant, the one who played with them, bonded with them, and taught them, whom they love the most, whose touch they crave?

I think it is important to understand that filial love is dependent and needful, with high expectations that you will provide for all needs and make every wrong thing right. If we do not take full responsibility for this love we have engendered, it could be dangerous. We must be as sensitive and attentive to our furry friend's moods as they are to ours, and we must avoid working with them if we are angry, fearful, anxious, or disoriented. They will detect such negative energy and assume it is directed at them. People unwilling to follow this rule run the risk of the aforementioned misunderstandings. This involves the dark side of limbic resonance – the norepinephorine circuit – which produces fear and defensiveness. If this happens, especially in the absence of sufficient flight distance, you could find yourself in an altercation with a natural warrior, armed with tremendous speed, agility, strength, plus 18 knives, and you lose.

Our detractors eagerly await such rare events so they can loudly proclaim their ridiculous self-aggrandizing propaganda. The animal has "reverted to the wild", thus proving that it never loved you. Should we also say that humans do not love because nearly every child bites its own mother, or because so many humans beat and kill their spouses, or because human altercations persist for whole decades involving whole nations of people deliberately making and using the most hideous weapons to blast each other to oblivion by the millions? No one who clings to the notion of human love after thousands of years of human atrocities should have any trouble believing that animals can love, need love, and deserve love.

I know there are animal trainers who will say that love has nothing to do with it. Probably because they have successfully trained animals that they did not love, and assumed the animal did not love them. This is like people skilled in the use of computers who have no idea how computers work. Most trainers will say you need a hand-reared animal. You cannot train a mother-raised adult animal. But still, they say its all about food – you become the source of food, and you induce the animal to work for their food. But the cognitive reasoning required to comprehend, accept, and execute this "food for work" program involves cerebral activity far more complex and unlikely than the filial love I have described. And it would be amazing indeed if wild cougar mothers had to be so cleaver as to devise all these training techniques because their babies did not love them. The principal of Occam's Razor tells us that the simplest explanation is the most probable. Which means that the animal love deniers are probably wrong. If so, they are utterly incapable of knowing and providing for the psychological needs of animals. And they should not control, legislatively or otherwise, how animals are cared for. This is one reason so many independent zoos refuse to join AZA with its autocratic rules against keepers forming affectionate relationships with animals. That kind of thinking may be good for a politically correct, monopolistic trade association, but it is not good for animals. That kind of thinking is the cruel and dangerous fallacy that produced Tatiana.

REFERENCES:

"Reward, Motivation and Emotion Systems Associated with Early-stage Intense Romantic Love", Journal of Neurophysiology, May 2005.

A General Theory of Love, 2000, Lewis, Amini, Larimon.

Empathy in Mental Illness, 2008 Farrow and Woodruff

The Wise Heart, 2008, Jack Kornfield

This article originally appeared in the journal of the Feline Conservation Federation, Volume 56, Issue 2 March/April 2012.

Mountain Lion Sighting

Forest Ranch Post, June 2009

Just wanted to let everyone in the Stage Road/Cabernet Way area know that we watched a large mountain lion in our back yard last night, May 17th. This lion did not seem afraid of us, or our large light shined in his face. He circled our yard for 5 or 10 minutes before moving off towards a neighbor's house.

My reply, 7-11-09

You are fortunate to have seen this magnificent cat in the Wild. I have never had the honor, even though I often hang out on my Land at night. My neighbor has: the cougar was strolling down the gravel road to our Land "like she owned the place" (ah, but she does!). Cougar-kitty has been here for 1 million years, after speciating out of the (now extinct) American cheetah (this is why the cubs have spots). Even the Original People (a.k.a. "Indians") have only been here 20,000 years. My neighbor has also seen the local brown bear up close, at 20 feet. We are on Doe Mill ridge, more remote than Stage Road/Cabernet Way.

WHY do people move to the back woods from the city, and then have a hissy-fit because critters live here? You or I could kill this poor kitty so easily (I assume you are armed like me). Give kitty a break. Maybe your property attracts deer, like mine.

The cougar is my totem animal, and you can be sure I have read every cougar book I can find. EVERY cougar attack on a human in the U.S. over the last 100 years has been METICULUOSLY recorded. Several books list every single one (there aren't very many), and one book is entirely devoted to the subject. You almost NEVER hear that in a single 7 year period (1997-2004), humans killed 30,000 cougars in the U.S. West. That is a large chunk of their entire population. Imagine cougars killing 10 MILLION humans in California, to put this in perspective.

Think of the cougar as a human male on all fours. We both evolved to take down the same prey. We are not each other's normal prey species. If cougars had somehow evolved on two legs, they would be built like a normal (Paleolithic) human male. Both species are the same size.

The males of the Original People here would ritually eat cougar flesh as a rite of passage, in order to incorporate the cougar's attributes. Likewise, a proper quiver had to be made out of cougar hide. These were acts of reverence. Cougar was not a normal part of the human diet.

Enclosed are some mountain lion sightings. (Pics of cougars hugging Bart)

News flash! Kitty terrorizes Hollywood.

(March 2013)

A 120 lb. male cougar fled the Santa Monica Mountains to avoid a territory fight with a larger male, managed to cross freeways without getting hit, and ended up in the Hollywood Hills, where he is now Terrorizing Tinseltown! Radio collars for kitty are just one front in the never-ending War on Terror!

A "homeless" story
(rednecks are tuff and self-reliant)

I could have been counted as homeless between 1994 and Aug. 2000, since I was living in a king-cab truck with a camper shell. This started when I had permanently damaged my back from working too hard as a landscaper, trying to save money for a home of my own while paying landlords (even then, the Bay Area had high rents). When I first moved into my truck, I could only lift 30 lbs. and work 15 hours a week, this condition lasted 9 months. I used my extremely modest savings to put 50% down on my Land, rather than let blood-sucking landlords take any more of it.

From not having to worry about money (which was at least 60% of my problem), and learning to rehabilitate/maintain my back, I recovered 70% of my original strength and stamina. 30% was permanent damage, never to be recovered. Kaiser, for all the premiums I was paying, was completely inept. After my first serious back injury in '91 (there were then 3 more), it took them 2 years to bother ordering a CAT scan to even see what was wrong, and 3 years to finally find me a competent physical therapist who taught me how to take care of myself. After a minor back strain that came as a warning, in June of '90, the doctor did not even bother asking me what I did for a living or how many hours I was working.

With most of my health back, I rebuilt my landscaping business, saving $8000 a year to pay off my Land and develop it with cash; this was done by early 1998. I also studied accounting as a 2nd occupation, and studied worker-owned/self-managed enterprises – out of which came one of the longer chapters in this book. The business kept growing, and in 1996, I took on an apprentice, helping him create a 30-hour a week job paying twice an hour what capitalists paid for equivalent work (NONE of this higher pay was a subsidy, my job as far as the accounting part went, was to assess how much wealth he was creating; any pay less than this is theft).

In the summer of 2000, I used a recent inheritance to put $36,000 down on a $56,000 top floor condo overlooking a big park and the big hills above Vallejo. More inherited wealth paid the $20,000 debt down to $9000 by 2002. By 2005, when health insurance premiums were eating me alive, and gas stayed well above $2.00 a gallon, I resumed camping in my truck part-time instead of commuting to Berkeley everyday (as of 2013, a commute costs me $20 a day, including bridge toll and wear-and-tear on my truck). I was now a "homeless" owner of 2 homes. Camping in town is illegal (just an infraction in Berkeley, but the police WILL rap on your door at 2AM if some uptight yuppie whines). This stupid law is not only a personal affront, it prevents me from cutting my NASTY greenhouse gas emissions by half.

Acknowledgements

First, to Albert Hoffman, discoverer of LSD, without which this book would never have been written. ("That NNNAasty LSD!")

To Mike Rubin, a friend of decades who read and critiqued my manuscript. Also Frank Runninghorse, Roger Wilkins and Alice Perrone. These friends disagree with me on a number of points. (Its SOO terrible, I just don't have yes-men in my life.) John Zerzan also read the early core chapters and encouraged me.

To my Mom, who did copy editing (but not content editing – she's not a radical).

To Bart Culver, who wrote most of the BAD KITTY chapter, and did not even charge me to reprint his writing. (I'm not the one who has lived with cougars for 25 years.)

To Richard Gibb, Doctor of Mental Health ("Doctor, NO!") who helped me with radical character reconstruction once a week from 1985 to 1989.

An invitation

Should this book do well, or even go big(*), I think it would be helpful to shine the starlight on OTHER PEOPLE who are part of the solution.

If you have successful experience putting into practice the solutions I have covered in this book, let me know. Even failures can be instructive and should be studied.

Let me know if you are interested in the rewilding sanctuary.

What has been called mystical experience is not possible to describe, but it is possible to speak from it to a limited degree. This will encourage others. It is not necessary for someone to have been given mystical experience to be part of the solution – motives are what count most. But the solution will require that many millions of people just here in America be given at least the level of experience I have been given. And not only once, but many times. Right motives are also what make this most possible.

I am a good speaker, and can be even more succinct/brief than I am in this book. If I have opportunity to speak, I'd prefer meeting in a circle with adequate time for questions and testimony from others. Unless this book does very well, I'll need reimbursement for travel expenses outside Northern California.

Contact info:

redpanther@intoedeninfo.com

Redpanther/John Burnett
1748 Tuolomne St., Box 21
Vallejo, CA94589

(*)And grandiose dreams are a dime-a-dozen here in America.